Don't Miss That
SALE

Home Performance-Based Selling

The No High Pressure Sales Methodogy

Arne Raisanen

DON'T MISS THAT SALE!
Home Performance-Based Selling
By Arne Raisanen

Copyright © 2014 Arne Raisanen

Publisher: Arne Raisanen

Book design: Nick Zelinger (www.nzgraphics.com)

ISBN: 978-0-9914289-0-8

First edition

Printed in the United States of America

CONTENTS

INTRODUCTION

Have you ever been on a sales call and everything is clicking? I mean really clicking! Your client is giving you those little yeses, you have overcome every objection with ease, and it's clear they see the value you're offering. You're convinced this sale is a sure thing! Your client agrees to everything: "Yes, that date will work...yes, those solutions sound great...yes, the investment seems worth it...and you came highly recommended." You even fill out all the paperwork. Then when it comes time to sign they say, "I love what you've shown me, but I'd like to sleep on it. Can I call you tomorrow?" And tomorrow never comes.

You follow up the next day and get voice mail. You leave a message and the client never calls back. What happened to your sure sale? As a professional, you want to do better next time, so you run the sales call through your head over and over, pondering what went wrong. It just doesn't add up. You did everything right. Or did you?

For the past 25 years, I've made my livelihood by working with people on a day-to-day basis, listening to their problems, and providing sound solutions. My experience comes from running a small contracting business and growing it to more than two million in sales. I like to say if a mistake could be made, I made it and learned a lot from it.

I didn't have a coach to guide me through my decisions or to show me the pitfalls I was about to experience. Today, my coaching has helped small businesses overcome these obstacles. Take Brad, a small business owner who had worked many years at a company as a service technician. One day the owner asked Brad if he would like to buy him out.

Brad bought the business, which had three employees and a couple of vans with some shop tools. Over the next 18 months, Brad saw the business dwindle. He ended up letting the three employees go. Then it was just Brad and his wife, who handled the incoming calls and bookkeeping.

Brad's biggest dilemma was that he had never trained in sales and didn't know how to charge for service. I went through the basics of setting some goals for where he should be, and plans for implementing them. I helped him to understand how his service really was an opportunity to educate the homeowner about practical solutions to correct the problem at hand. I explained to Brad that if he followed the steps I put in place he would see instant results.

When I looked up, Brad had tears in his eyes. It was like, "Finally this makes sense!" The next afternoon I received an e-mail from him.

> *Arne,*
> *Just wanted to let you know, we just scheduled our*
> *first Negative Home Pressure test. Thank you for*
> *your help!!*
> *Brad*

Since then, I've traveled across America meeting business owners who are looking for solutions to a wide variety of business-related stumbling blocks. I've discovered that many have tried different programs meant to solve the issues they're facing, but all too often those programs don't work, leaving the business owner struggling. Often the owners fall back into their old habits, doing what they're comfortable with, only to get frustrated with the lack of support from their investment.

Most programs cost a lot of money up front, with a lot of promises about how they will work but very little training in implementation. Often an investment in consulting is too big for a small contractor to absorb. Mostly, it's just too overwhelming for a contractor to overcome the cost versus implementation time. Don't get me wrong, many of these programs can work, it's just that they're designed for larger companies.

This book is the first step to building the big-picture perspective for small business owners who want to grow profitable, with the satisfaction of knowing they're making a significant difference in their customers' lives. You're an entrepreneur who has taken the leap and started a business. That tells me you're a goal setter, action taker, and builder with a vision for success. No doubt you've already made many strategic moves to grow your business.

There wasn't an obvious need for your business, so you needed to create a reason why someone would want what you were offering.

Like many of us specializing in the home service industry, you may have started out as a technician with a talent for repairing things like furnaces, air conditioners, plumbing, and electrical systems. You probably had a passion for customer service. Now you have taken your passion and poured it into a business, building value for your customers, showing them why they should hire you and trust you.

Consumers, in general, are skeptical of anything new and definitely do not want to be strong-armed or pressured into making a hasty decision. This prompts many of them to do research via the Internet. Oftentimes, when you give a proposal to install new equipment for   potential or existing customers, you may be surprised at their knowledge about the features and benefits of the equipment.

By the time they call you, consumers have researched all the different products on the market and pretty much know what a new furnace, heat pump, air conditioner, water heater, or electrical service will cost. In reality, the pricing or products they've found might not be right for their needs, but nevertheless they have a price to compare to yours. The bottom line is that the sale is often based on price.

This puts you in the position of either lowering your price or offering some other free service to get the job. This situation has you searching for ways to generate more revenue to offset your losses, and may have prompted you to pick up this book.

I want to make it very clear: the methods I'm about to share with you are not about getting rich quick, and my goal is not to give you a magic power for making money. Instead, I'm offering you the tools that will set you apart from your competitors, increase your profits, increase the size of the jobs you contract, and fill in your slow seasons. The more you put into it, the more you will get out of it. Make no doubt about it, the work will be hard, but the rewards will be worth it.

If you want to grow your business, here's what you should be wondering about the plan I'm sharing with you:

"Will it increase my closing ratios?"

"Will it increase my profit margins?"

"Will it increase customer satisfaction?"
"Will it decrease problem call-backs and frivolous warranty work?"

The answer to all of those questions is, "Yes it will!"
I've learned that most contractors regularly walk right past hundreds of thousands of dollars of business every day. That's right, opportunities are likely staring you right in the face today, but you're just not seeing them! The HVAC business alone offers these opportunities:

- **The indoor air quality market in the U.S. represents a market of more than seven billion dollars.** (*US Indoor Air Quality Market Report*)

- **Nine out of ten homes in America have indoor air quality problems.** (*Department of Energy*)

- **That's over 90% of your customers!**

Have you noticed that most sales systems being taught today seem canned and impersonal? What's in it for the customer is not even considered. Your customers are real people with real problems. They're part of your community, and you can help them in a positive way. You need to know the solutions, present them with integrity, and communicate the value of what you're doing for them—*without being pushy or critical.* All too many sales approaches come across as reproachful: "If only you had done this before…It's a big mistake to do that…Here's what you don't understand…" That approach is a *big turn-off.* Customers don't call you because they want you to tell them their problems. They want

5

a professional to offer them solutions that will give them confidence that they've called the right person, so they can move on with their lives without frustration or worry.

Think about it. You're on a service call for a problem; let's say it's a failed air conditioner. The immediate fix is to replace a burnt-out contactor. That's easy! It will get the cooling back on, but it's an inexpensive repair. To make matters worse, you've already lowered your service-call rate just to get the homeowner to agree to hire you. Other sales programs have taught you that you need to find other issues so you can create more work, right? That's what the so-called sales experts often tell you: Go in with a low entry-price as a lead in, find other potential problems, and use high pressure tactics to create a bigger ticket.

So you tell the homeowner, "I found that the contactor on your outdoor unit is burnt," and you even bring her to the outdoor unit to show him your findings. You're trying to build credibility, which I'll agree is important. You explain what the charge will be to get it back on line doing its job of cooling the home. So the homeowner agrees to the repair. So far so good, right? But now the up-selling begins:

"Mrs. Homeowner, I was looking over your system and it's over 10 years old. That blower motor on your air handler could go out at any time. Since I'm already here today, we could take care of this now. It would save you another service call, plus I can give you a ten percent discount. You wouldn't want this to go out on the hottest day of the year, would you?"

Many times the homeowner will agree, because you're the expert. And you may think you succeeded, because you did create a bigger ticket. But if you think that's a successful transaction, I beg to differ, because that kind of transaction does not help the customer out. You emptied her wallet of some hard-earned money, and when her husband gets home there's a good chance he'll call you for further explanation. The next time they need service, I bet they'll do more research before hiring any contractor. And they probably won't hire you again. So you've lost a potential long-term revenue stream from that customer, you've lost the word-of-mouth advertising they might have generated with better service, and you may have even gained some negative advertising as they spread the word—potentially costing you even more customers.

Back in the 1990s, I was subcontracting installation work for a gas company that sold equipment to its customers. My company would change out a furnace or air conditioner for a flat labor rate. We were changing out equipment every week, sometimes twice a day! At first, I was pleased with the work. Then I noticed an odd pattern. Often the customers were either older retired couples or young and inexperienced homeowners. Often the old equipment we removed seemed to be working just fine.

I started asking the homeowners why they were having a new furnace or air conditioner installed. What was their motivation? The answer I received most of the time was not encouraging: "The gas company said we need a new system!" Oh, the gas company had it all figured out. They even offered to finance the new equipment by adding the cost to the customer's monthly gas bill. I ended up dropping that gas company account for one simple reason: *I could not be part of a scam.*

Offering practical, honest solutions to homeowners is much more profitable for contractors than misleading marketing, pushy sales tactics, or impersonal service that doesn't focus on the customer. Being a true problem solver, and not a "Band-Aid" contractor, will help you better retain your existing customers, which is far easier than finding new ones. What's more, word-of-mouth from those satisfied customers will help you add new customers, too.

The man who succeeds has a program.
He fixes his course and adheres to it. He lays
his plans and executes them. He goes straight
to his goal. He knows where he wants to go
and he knows that he's going to get there.
He loves what he's doing and loves the journey
that is taking him to the objects of his desires.
He is bubbling over with enthusiasm and he is
filled with zeal. This is a man who succeeds.
— Anonymous

If you're a progressive-thinking contractor, you'll be excited to know that the system I'm sharing with you does not rely on the economy, new home building, mild weather, or price-driven box sales! Instead I've created a customer-oriented system that will revolutionize the way you go to market as a small business owner, salesperson, or contractor—forever.

The good news is that you can implement this system at any point in your operation, whether your company is brand new or has been passed down through generations. It's never too late. Every business starts with a dream. You just need to reconnect with that dream and turn it into solid, practical, actionable goals that will grow a business you can be proud of. The system you're about to learn is a set of interlocking processes that all complement each other:

- **You'll learn how to set actionable goals.**

- **You'll learn how to write and implement a business plan that will move you toward your goals.**

- **You'll learn how to write a budget that will fuel your plan and keep it realistic with regard to spending, billing, and timing.**

- **You'll learn how to conduct marketing that helps you to increase sales.**

- **You'll learn how to conduct sales and service that help you to maintain and expand your customer base.**

- **In turn your sales will help take you toward your goal.**

All those steps add together to create my business building system, which can now become your system. It has worked for me, and for every company I've trained that has actually used it. So if you're ready to do the work, let's get started!

Chapter 1

Make Your Dreams Reality by Setting Goals

"Some of the greatest dreams never become reality
for one simple reason: no plan."
– Arne Raisanen

Many people think they have goals, when often what they really have are dreams, and that's a very different thing. Dreaming is vital to inspiring people to create goals, but a dream is not a goal. A goal is specific and defined, with a plan for how to reach it, steps for implementation, and measurements for success. Goal setting is vital to your success in every aspect of your business. I can't give you a dream, but I don't need to—if you have your own business, then you already have a dream. What many small business owners fail to understand is that they'll never achieve their dreams without establishing goals. And that's something I can tell you how to do. Some people might be tempted to skip goal setting because they believe it's a wishy-washy feel-good concept that has little to do with the step-by-step reality of running a successful business. I assure you that nothing else in your system will work well if you don't first learn how to set and implement goals. Goal setting will help you understand all the other aspects of creating a successful business that I'm going to lay out in this book.

Even if your business has been around for a long time, it's never too late to work on goal setting. Most of the time contractors are so busy being busy that the days and weeks go by without them moving an inch toward their dreams. Their days get eaten up by tasks and emergencies, until their dreams get away from them. All this can be avoided if you learn the process of setting and keeping goals.

I've coached many business owners and salespeople to set goals that have come to fruition. So I'm going to talk to you as your coach. The goal-setting process I'll explain in this chapter will focus on business goals, but you can also apply it to personal goals. Without a goal, you can't create the main thing your business will need to succeed: a plan. But the goal comes first, so let's start there.

Why Set Goals?

One of the biggest objections that small business owners make when I coach them is that they see goal setting as a waste of time. They believe they already know what they want, and they just want to get to it. In reality, for most of them setting a goal has never been more than a fleeting thought or a dream they've talked about. They do not understand how incredibly important a goal is and how it can tangibly impact the future of their entire business. It's the foundation for everything else, and since you work in houses you surely know that without a foundation, the whole structure will fall.

Let me tell you, I can understand why people don't want to face this seemingly simple task; something inside them knows that it's not as simple as it seems. It's very difficult to sit down and write down your goals on a piece of paper or type them into a Word document. If it were easy, everyone would do it. It takes time and effort to set and achieve goals. By applying yourself to this task, you will already be doing something that sets your business apart.

It's only human nature to be tempted to avoid things we don't like to do, and it's easy to convince yourself that goal setting isn't something you need. You vividly remember the day you went into business, and neither you nor anybody else said anything about goal setting. You were seized by the entrepreneurial spirit, so you hung your shingle out and got to work. If you're still in business, you figure you must be doing something right. You just want to start from here, not go back and start over.

But think about what has happened to you since that first exciting day working for yourself. Somehow the excitement of getting off the ground became the daily grind of work. Often it's work you don't understand, work you don't want to do, and work nobody ever told you that you would have to do. I'm here to tell you that a lot of that agony will go away if you'll accept one thing and take action on it: A solid business requires a solid system in place that will gauge your success, and that system starts with a goal.

Although goal setting isn't easy, it is exciting. You need not look at this as a chore. This is what is going to light the fire under your dream, so it will take off like a rocket. So if you think about it, goal setting should be one of the highlights of setting your business up, or of resetting your business if it's already underway. It's never too late, even if you're an established business owner who has never set goals, or who has half-heartedly jotted down some dreams but never done anything more with them. Goal setting should be an inspiring moment in your thought process, as you envision your dream and then establish the path to make it real.

I can tell you without a doubt that most successful business owners set goals every day: both short-term goals and long-term goals. Goal setting is one of the reasons for their success. I guarantee you they don't wake up in the morning and say, "I wonder what I'll be doing today," or "I wonder what's up for next week," or even "I wonder what we'll be doing next month." Successful business owners project goals well in advance, and then plan agendas and lay out strategies for how they'll execute those goals.

Setting goals helps you get past the monotony of all the picky little day-to-day details that can drag you off track. It helps keep you focused on what is important to the long-term success of your business. Without goals, you run from one entrepreneurial seizure to another, getting worked up over this and that, but accomplishing nothing. Knowing your way around products and services, having experience in your field, and having a great work ethic are important, but they are not enough for success. You have to know exactly what you want to achieve long term, what you plan to do day-by-day to achieve it, and how you'll know when you get there. You can apply all the energy, experience, and enthusiasm in the world to your work, but if you don't have specific goals, you're just going to create mass confusion. Where will you and your business be headed then? Right off the rails! If you don't know where you're going, you're heading for a train wreck.

Although setting goals is not easy, it *is* pretty straightforward. For the best results you should be writing down what you want to accomplish in the next thirty days, the next six months, the next twelve months, the next three years, and the next five years.

Of course, if you just write your goals down and don't know what to do about them, you're definitely not going to accomplish them. So for every goal you write down, you also need to write down an action plan. Again, this is pretty simple: a goal is all about going from point A to point B, and the action plan is how you plan to accomplish that. A goal can be short term or long term. The short-term goals usually have fewer steps in their action plans, while long-term goals have more steps—and sometimes those steps include a series of short-term goals.

Let's say your goal is to have three million dollars in the bank when you reach retirement age. If that's what you really want, you had better have a plan of how you're going to make that happen. It's definitely not going to happen all by itself. No one else will do it but you.

Remember, when setting goals, it's not enough just to write down, "I want to have three million dollars when I retire." That's a wish. A goal must include your action plan for how you're going to do it.

Although you can set goals by yourself, I've found that people have greater momentum and success when they find a coach or mentor to help them set their goals. A coach brings an objective viewpoint to the process, and can help you uncover the hidden fears and the misconceptions that may be standing between you and your goals.

Once you've set your goals, does that mean they're certain to become reality? No. That's why they're called goals, not guarantees. Life can throw all kinds of curve balls at you. With a goal there are no guarantees, but with no goal, there is one guarantee: you won't achieve much. Here's the thing about goals: even if you fail, as long as you keep resetting new goals, you will achieve something. It may not look exactly the way you thought it would, but if you keep heading in the direction you intend to go, you're bound to get somewhere.

Look at Thomas Edison. His goal was to build an electric light bulb. Did he succeed the first time? Shoot no! In fact, he missed the mark thousands of times. But he never called those failures; instead he said: *"I have not failed. I've just found 10,000 ways that won't work."* Talk about perseverance!

You have to be motivated to make goals happen. And you need to have clarity as to how you will achieve them.

Step by Step

Let's lay the groundwork for goal setting. Remember, you really should have someone help you establish your goals. Having that objective eye on the process and having someone to help hold you accountable will only increase your success level.

Your first step is to write down a list of five or six goals that are pertinent to your success.

I've put together a sample list of goals below to show you how to start. Whether your goals are professional or personal, your list will be unique to you, your needs, and your dreams. If you have no idea what your goals might be, and don't know where to start, this is where a mentor or coach would come in, asking you questions to help you figure out what is important to you.

Sample List of Goals

1. Overcoming low-bid competitors who take our jobs
2. Solutions to slow or money-losing periods due to mild weather
3. Ways to increase consumer satisfaction
4. New ways to generate referral business
5. Ways to increase net profit

Your next step is to create a chart for your goals and rate your current level of satisfaction with how close you are to achieving each goal on a scale of 0 to 4, 0 being very unsatisfied, and 4 being thoroughly satisfied. (This can be done on a grid paper, Microsoft word, or Xcel.) This chart will serve as an indicator for which of your goals need the most work and in what order you need to prioritize them.

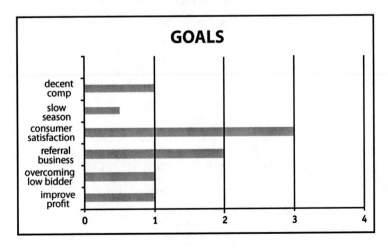

Once you've established your goal chart, you can move on to the next step and list your goals in order of their importance to you. Then, if you don't have a coach, you need to ask yourself why your progress on each goal does or doesn't need improvement. Write reasons down for each goal, so you understand what needs to happen with that goal for you to make progress.

Next, you're going to establish time periods for your goals, based on their order of importance. Your most important goal should be a short-term goal, and you should give it something like 30 to 90 days to achieve improvement. Your second most important goal could be a three to six-month goal, and so on. You may want to bundle some related goals that you plan to accomplish together. As a coach, I've discovered that most business goals tend to complement each other. In other words, when you achieve success at one, you tend to move closer to the others as well.

Your next step is to decide on your action plan: the steps you'll take to reach your goals, and the standards of measurement you'll use to know when you've achieved success. For this step, get out a pencil and paper, and be prepared to answer the list of questions in the next section, *Setting Goals*. If you're acting as your own coach, just remember to be honest with yourself. Before you ask yourself the first question, make sure to tell yourself, "This is my future and I want to succeed." Shoot, go ahead and write that at the top of your sheet:

_____

This is my future and I want to succeed.

_____

Okay, let's dig in…

Setting Goals

If I were coaching you through turning your list of goals into an action plan, I would structure our first session as an interview. It would go something like this:

- **Coach:** What goal in your business would you like to achieve over the next 90 days?
- **You:** *Answer*

- **Coach:** I'm curious. Explain to me what achieving this goal means to you? Be specific. How will you feel? What will it look like to you?
- **You:** *Answer*

- **Coach:** When you achieve this goal, what tangible evidence will you have to prove to you that you've achieved it? What will it feel like?
- **You:** *Answer*

- **Coach:** Where and with whom do you want to accomplish this goal?
- **You:** *Answer*

- **Coach:** What actions are you willing to take to achieve this goal?
- **You:** *Answer*

- **Coach:** When you achieve this goal, what will be the impact on other aspects of your business?
- **You:** *Answer*

- **Coach:** Thinking back, what roadblocks have gotten in the way of you achieving this goal in the past?
- **You:** *Answer*

- **Coach:** What action steps will you take to acquire these new resources?
- **You:** *Answer*

- **Coach:** Let's select completion dates for each goal, based on your charts.
- **You:** *Uh-oh, this is serious!*

That's right, now we get serious. Your dreams are now on their way to becoming a reality. When people see their goals on paper, often the first thing that strikes them is the thrilling, scary notion, "Wow! Can this really happen?"

Yes, it can, but only if you follow through with it all the way to the end. Many will expect a quick fix, and when it doesn't happen right away they'll give up and go back to their old ways. Those folks will find themselves back to struggling and struggling with no end in sight. There is no quick fix. If there were, you would already have heard about it and started doing it.

Your action plan doesn't mean you'll never face any more problems or challenges. You'll continue to run into roadblocks as you move toward your goals. The only big difference between successful people and unsuccessful people is that the successful ones don't let roadblocks stop them. They simply see problems and setbacks as an opportunity to adjust their plan and come up with new solutions.

I remember a marketing dilemma I once faced in my business, which I definitely saw as a major roadblock. Our direct mailers were not working, consumers were not calling, and things had to change. So my colleagues and I started brainstorming, and we came up with the idea of putting on free seminars to educate consumers on the whole-house concept of building science. We then studied how we would accomplish this goal.

Here was the scariest part: I was elected to be the key speaker for the seminars. I want to make something clear: I had never done public speaking before, so I was really stepping outside the box. I was so far out of the box that I could not even see the box! So I prepared like crazy, to help increase my assurance that even if I made a fool of myself at least I'd give everyone the right information. I sweated bullets during the presentation, but I did it. I made a plan, and I followed it through.

And let me tell you: that seminar was a great success, and the beginning of many more successes to come. One side benefit was that I learned how to do public speaking, which has led to my success at many other goals.

The bottom line: Goal setting can and will help you achieve wonderful things which will bring you closer to your goal, and even beyond...

A dream will always be a dream if you don't write it down. Most dreams are never put into a plan and will fade away and be long forgotten.

Chapter 2

Your Business Won't Fly Without a Plan

*Create a definite plan for carrying out your desire
and begin at once, whether you are ready or not,
to put this plan into action*
– Napoleon Hill

Whether you are a business owner or a salesperson, this book is for you. Actually a business owner is still, at bottom, a salesperson. Both get paid only after the sale is completed.

A business owner does have a bit more outlay to contend with than a salesperson. He or she must have a budget for advertising, a budget for marketing—which is not the same as advertising—and above all a business plan.

Many small businesses start with one person's dream: the dream of no longer answering to others and instead becoming your own boss, the dream of working fewer hours, or just the dream of doing your own thing and creating something new. Some new business owners tell me they simply grew sick and tired of making so much money for their boss or employer, and wanted to keep some of it for themselves. Mostly they just have the independent, entrepreneurial spirit that is so strong in America. With that, a new business is born.

The sad part is that within the first year, 40% of those excited entrepreneurs will be out of business. Over the next five years 80% of them will have failed. Why such a high failure rate? According to Dun & Bradstreet, 80% of small businesses fail because they cannot maintain cash flow.

Most dreams are just that: dreams. If the dreamer does not create and implement a detailed, actionable plan, the dream disappears into thin air. Think of yourself as an airline pilot. A pilot will never take off without first choosing a destination to land, and creating and filing a flight plan to get there. If you don't have a plan, your business will crash.

I have talked to many small business owners over the past 25 years. The majority started a business because they knew the technical side of the trade. But they knew nothing about the business side of their trade, or about the way any kind of business is run. Most of them did not understand what a financial statement was or how to create a budget. Very few had written down their goals. Some maybe had a ten-year goal in mind, but no short-term goals that would take them there, no step-by-step process figured out by which they planned to reach their ten-year goal. They had a destination with no flight plan. They were bound to go off course.

Your plan must take into account more than just the equipment, skills, and people you need to do the job you envision. You must also think of exactly how you are going to handle advertising, marketing, customer service, sales, cash flow, and more. You must think of it all not just in terms of what you hope will happen, but what you'll do to ensure things happen the way you want, and what contingency plans you'll have in place in case they don't. You need to ensure that you know how to do everything in a way that balances your cash in and cash out, so that the revenue stream flows in your favor.

The long and the short of it is this: if you don't have a business plan and you're not setting goals, your chances of failure increase one hundredfold. You need to have a clear plan written down on paper, complete with daily tasks and time set aside to accomplish these tasks. As a small business owner, you're now also a CEO, CFO, sales consultant, and much more. Some people have to juggle so much that they don't think they have the time to write down a budget, but they're looking at it backward. With so many balls to juggle, you must have a budget, or all those balls are going to come tumbling down.

When I talk about a budget, I don't mean jotting down a few figures at the beginning of the year, which you put in a drawer and never look at again. I'm talking about a working budget: a live system that goes from month to month and follows your financial statement.

Over the years, I've talked to many owners of small businesses that are doing three-quarter million in sales a year, which sounds great. But many of them are heading for disaster because of their lack of budgeting. I typically ask the question, "So what is your budget for advertising this year?" Typically I get a blank stare. The biggest reason you put a budget together is to know where your money's coming from and where your money's going. Money is always moving in a constant current; that's why they call it currency. If you are not in control of that flow, your money will disappear. It's just a matter of time. Once that happens, your dream of owning a business will become a living nightmare.

Some who learn the hard way about planning and budgeting end up shutting their businesses down out of frustration. Other businesses do have a business plan, but shut their doors anyway because they're tired of getting beaten by price. Profit has become a foreign word in their company, and they don't know how to turn it around even though they have a plan. They fear that if they raise prices they'll lose more customers, and they can't afford to lower prices because they'll dive into the red. So they give up.

Eleven Steps to Your Business Blueprint

A business plan is not just a bunch of ideas in your head, and it's not just a budget—though that's part of it. A business plan is a complete assessment of where your company is now, where you want to be in the future, and what you plan to do to get there. A business plan sets the overall purpose and goal of your company. As you follow my suggestions to create your own plan, don't get caught up in those details that don't help you. The primary objective is to define a clear direction that you want to move in.

Remember, a plan not only includes a series of things to do, but also addresses the purpose, or ultimate desired outcome, for all that you do. That purpose can be changed or modified if necessary. That's why it's called a *plan*, and not a rulebook. Maybe a better word is a blueprint: a blueprint for your business, how you want it to develop, and what you hope to see it become in the future.

It's very important that your blueprint not just be something you carry in your head. If you want a real business plan, you must put it into writing.

With that in mind, let's consider how to shape your blueprint, step by step:

Step One: Who You Are. It's important to clearly identify who and what your business is. Who are the officers? What type of company is it: a Sole Proprietorship, a Limited Liability Company, a Corporation? Where is your business physically located? What is the primary purpose of your business? For example, you might define your services like this: *Super Duper Services is a residential service heating and plumbing company that primarily works with homeowners.* Having a true definition of your company and its purpose will help you focus the rest of your plan.

Step Two: What You Sell. For example: *Super Duper Services is a service-based company that sells exceptional service while also providing heating and plumbing products.* Making clear exactly what you provide customers will keep you on track, so that everything you do traces back to why you went into business in the first place. That's something you don't want to ever lose track of. So, for example, if your company provides heating, plumbing, or electrical services, then you definitely wouldn't want to start a carpet division in your business, would you? You might laugh and say, "Who would do that?" I can tell you from experience that it does happen. But it shouldn't, because it can really take away from your ability to shine at what you're good at. It can also waste a lot of your time and cost you money. But once your plan defines who your company is, it tells you where to draw your route and destination. How can you get there, if you don't know where *there* is?

Step Three: SWOT Analysis. That is, you need to identify your company's strengths, weaknesses, opportunities, and threats.

SWOT

S = your strengths

W = your weaknesses

O = your opportunities

T = threats you are facing

A SWOT analysis will help you go beyond identifying who and what your company is and what it does, to identifying its capabilities and assets, as well as its problems and liabilities, not only financially speaking, but on the whole. With this analysis you are trying to identify those things that will keep you moving forward on the road toward your company goals, as well as those little road blocks that might stop you or force you to change direction along the way.

Let's assume for a minute that you're a great technician who has a vast knowledge of all the aspects of repairing a piece of equipment. This would be a strength, right? But on the flip side, let's say that when you try to communicate this knowledge to your customer you start talking like you have marbles in your mouth. That would be a weakness.

The S and W, or strengths and weakness, are about you and your company. Meanwhile, the O and T, or opportunities and threats, are about things outside of your company that you cannot control but that nonetheless have the power to impact your business. One opportunity would be that 90% of your market has indoor air quality problems. That's not something your company created; it's just a reality that's out there, but your company will vastly benefit from harvesting that potential. On the other hand, one threat would be competitors who have a bigger market share and who are doing a better job than you at taking care of the market.

Your SWOT analysis is one exercise that you should definitely do with a coach or mentor, for the simple reason that four eyes are better than two. As business owners, we sometimes don't realize when we have blinders on, ignoring brutal facts because we fear what it will take to address reality. If someone doesn't rip off those blinders, you may well be doomed to failure. Remember, the difference between a good company and a great company is that the great company faces the truth of what's facing its business, even when the truth hurts.

Step Four: Know Your Market. Knowing the area where you're marketing is critical to the growth of your business. If you don't know who you're marketing to, then it will be very hard to know what to market or what results to expect. In this step you will research and define your market area's demographics:

Your Market's Demographics

Who lives in your market area?
What is the typical age of people in your market area?
What is the median income in your market area?
What is the average age of the homes?
What is the percentage of home ownership?
How long are people staying in their homes?
What is the buying pattern?

Sometimes you can research demographics from past newspaper articles, census bureau information, or online sources, but you can also do plenty of useful research on your own. For example, take a cruise around your neighborhood and check out the condition of the homes and the vehicles in the driveways. Are there a lot of new cars or are most of them five to ten years old? Do you see a lot of nicely landscaped yards or are most of them run down? These are telltale signs of how the people in your market are spending their residual money, or if they even have any to spend.

Step Five: Sales Forecast. Creating a sales forecast can be more of an art than a science. In the previous step we talked about your market area, which ties into your sales forecast. The easiest way to start this step is to break it down by department, and then further break each department into types of sales. For example, in your service department you can break projected sales figures into: plan maintenance sales, clean-and-tune service calls, emergency-demand calls, and regular non-emergency calls. In your product sales department, you can break projected sales figures into: heating sales, cooling sales, and indoor air quality sales.

To give you the clearest picture, it's important to segment sales figures for each department into 12 one-month cycles. Remember, by projecting sales, you're deciding what numbers to enter into your live, working budget. For example, if your sales for July are projected at $100K, then you need a plan to generate that kind of income. That brings us to the next step...

Step Six: Marketing Plan. If you want to make sales, you need clients to sell to. If you want clients to sell to, you need a marketing plan. In Chapter 3, I'll explain how your marketing campaign should work. A marketing plan is what turns opportunity into reality, a call for an estimate into a paid test, a paid test into a product sale. You must begin by knowing that the world will keep on turning with or without your business. This is why it's critical for you to communicate to your customers why they need you; that is, why they're better off with your services than without them, and why they want to hire you and not your competitor. Your marketing plan will create opportunities for you to get in front of potential clients, which brings us to the next step in your business plan...

Step Seven: Sales Strategy. Having a sales system that complements your marketing plan will strengthen your ability to reach your sales forecast. If your sales forecast for July is $100K in gross sales, then you need a strategy to make that happen. This step right here is where many businesses fall down. Here's why:

Super Duper Services starts a marketing campaign featuring a special spring clean-and-tune for an entry-level price. The intention is that these leads will turn into bigger jobs and increased sales. At first it seems to work great: the campaign does bring leads into Super Duper's service department. But that's where things fall apart, because the service department was never instructed on how to turn this service call into an opportunity lead. So the technician runs the call like he usually does, doing only the advertised clean-and-tune and never offering further testing. At the end of the campaign, Super Duper's owner looks at his numbers and realizes he actually lost money. He goes back to the marketing department and says, "That campaign failed. We need to try something else." But in reality, the campaign did work. The marketing system made the phone ring, and you had the lead. *It was your sales strategy that failed!* In Chapter 6, I'll show you how to complement your marketing plan with a step-by-step strategy for running successful service and sales calls.

Step Eight: Team Responsibilities. Whether you own a small company in which you wear all the hats, or a large company with multiple departments, you still need to know what each team member and each department is responsible for. In your business plan, it's important to define departments and job titles, and create a clear description of the responsibilities of each. That may include, but is not limited to: the Chief Executive Officer (CEO), Chief Financial Officer (CFO), sales manager, service manager, service tech, customer service, accounting, human resources, etc.

Think about this: what if your plan succeeds? Your company is growing, your marketing is complementing sales, your sales ratios are increasing, and profits are going up. Everything is humming along, but you, who have been running multiple positions, are getting a little overwhelmed. You're at the point where you need to bring in a manager to run your service department. So you find a qualified manager and bring her into the fold.

You're relieved that you're going to have a little time to breathe, and your new manager is excited to show you what she can do. She asks you what you expect from her, and you say something like, "Just take care of the service department so I don't have to. I'm too busy doing everything else for this business." A month later you're looking at your financial statements and you notice that your service department revenue has dropped. You're alarmed to see that your profit has disappeared. So you go back to your new manager to find out what happened.

Within minutes you can see that your manager has pushed off to the wayside many of the systems you worked so hard to implement. You're livid. So you start ranting, "Why didn't this get done? How come this isn't being filled out? Why aren't these customers taken care of?" Your manager is bewildered, saying, "I didn't know you wanted me to do that. You never told me to fill that out. I didn't know that was a priority." If you're smart, that's when a remembered voice will echo in your head: "Just take care of the service department so I don't have to. I'm too busy doing everything else for this business." Then whose fault is this really? Yours!

Your system failed because your manager didn't know how to put your plan into place. And the manager didn't even know what she didn't know, because you never established written responsibilities for the service department.

If you make that kind of mistake, it's going to cost you a boatload of money and lost time. You may even lose a good manager if you don't give that person the tools to manage. So, regardless of the size of your business today, think about the future and write a detailed description of the responsibilities and tasks of each department and each position.

Step Nine: Profit and Loss. As a business owner, you need to have a clear understanding of your profit and loss statement. Not only how to write one and read one, but also how critical a lifeline it is for your success. If you don't know how much money you're making, how much you're losing, where it's coming from, and where it's going, then how can you steer the rest of your plan in the right direction?

I'm astounded by how often I meet small business owners who don't know their numbers. In my coaching interviews, I ask some very basic, but important questions involving profit and loss, such as: "What is your cost of goods, in terms of percentages? What is your gross profit margin? What are your sales projections for next month? What are your closing ratios in your sales department? What is your cost per lead today? What percentage of your budget do you spend on advertising?" Without the answers, we cannot make any kind of plan.

But more often than not, the owner just gives me a deer-in-the-headlights look, and one blanket answer that goes something like this: "Arne, I'm not sure. I'm so busy I let my accountant keep track of all that for me. My accountant lets me know at the end of the year if I need to change anything."

"Really?!" I say. "You're letting your accountant run your business?"

Not that I have anything against accountants, but what do they know about your business? Sure, they understand how to read a P&L statement, but only from a reactive standpoint! An accountant knows your numbers, but has no day-to-day knowledge of your business, its operation, its people, its purpose, its goals, its capabilities, or its opportunities. Accountants are a great help when tax time comes, but they aren't in business to make your business run the best it can. They can read the numbers, but only you can translate those numbers into indications of problems that need solving or opportunities that need developing. They can tell you if your business is in the red or in the black, but they can't tell you how to use your profit and loss statement to help you plan a budget.

If you don't understand a P&L, your chances of failure are high. Instead of creating a realistic live budget, you will go from one dilemma to another. So make sure you create a detailed profit and loss statement that tells you where your money is coming from and where it's going. And make sure you know how it tracks every type of revenue your business makes or spends. You'll need that P&L in hand for the next step.

Step Ten: The Bottom-Up Budget. In most typical budgets, the business owner is paid last, but I like to turn that upside down, and pay the owner first. That's why I call it the Bottom-Up Budget. It's great to have a sense of responsibility, which is why most owners first pay the vendors, the taxes, the rent, the light bill, the insurance company, their employees, and so on, before they pay themselves a dime. And sometimes a dime isn't far off from what's left. But a budget is a plan, not a result, and the budget process is our chance to plan for different results. So, I use a Bottom-up Budget, in which I plan on paper to pay myself first. This allows me to decide how much I want or need, and then to work the rest of my plan to make it happen. Remember, if I plan it, the chances are high it will happen.

Setting a budget is probably the task small business owners dread most. One reason you went into business for yourself was so you could do your own thing, not spend hours sitting around doing paperwork and following procedures. Shoot! That might even be what you hated most about working for someone else! But if you don't write that budget, you may not be doing your own thing for long. Businesses without clear budgets are prone to failure.

I invite you to think about this from a different angle. Let's say that during your first year in business your gross sales are $100K with a net profit of 5%. That means you keep $5,000. Not much, but not bad for a first year. Then let's suppose that the next year you do $150K in gross sales, but you had a few bad jobs, so your bottom line is actually worse than last year. Let's call it a loss of 5%, or $7,500. But you're an optimist, so you say, "No worries, I can make that up in a couple months!" The third year in business, at first it looks as if your rosy prediction was right: you're cranking the work out and hitting some home runs, you hire your first employee, the cash is moving through your fingers, and you hit the $300K mark! So you think things are looking up, until you go over your P&L statement and discover you're still losing 5%. This time that means $15,000 lost. Five percent just became a big number, didn't it?

How is that possible?

Plenty of new business owners make the mistake of not even bothering to answer that question. Instead they have this thought: "I'm just going to have to work harder next year to overcome the loss." But that's what they did last year! So the crazy cycle starts all over: selling more work and hiring more employees, until the 5% loss becomes $50,000 and the cash runs out! At that point they're broke, they're done; it's over.

That's why you absolutely must set up a budget. One of the first things people notice when they switch from flying by the seat of their pants to writing a budget is that there's this little thing they've been forgetting, called overhead. If you're not covering your overhead, then your expenses are going to exceed your income.

A budget helps you make solid decisions before you make a move, before you hire an employee, buy a new vehicle, or purchase new equipment. Think about how much more freedom from worry you'll feel next year if you've already decided where all the money is going, and you've already planned to pay yourself first. Now you know how much you'll be making, how much you'll be paying for advertising, how much insurance will cost, how much your supply bills will run, what you'll spend in fuel, how much rent will be, and so on.

The most important thing your budget should address is what your projected sales have to be in order for your business to end the year with a profit and not a loss. The second most important thing it will address is what you need to produce on average every day to meet your budget. The third most important thing it will address is detailing the true overhead costs required for you to do business, so that when you're bidding a job you know the right percentages you need to make to bring in a profit.

Your overhead will be at least the same percentage of your budget as the overhead of the 30-man shop down the road. In fact, if your business is smaller your overhead may be higher.

The moment you know your overhead is the moment you take control of your money. For instance, maybe you're so overloaded with work you want to hire a new employee, but you're not sure you can afford one. Now that you have a written budget, all you have to do is enter the wages and costs of a new employee into your budget and see how the rest of the figures change. You'll see immediately how much your overhead will increase, and how much more revenue you'll need to bring in to cover that additional overhead. If you can make the revenue to cover it, then go hire that employee!

A few months ago a business owner called me to say he was ready to hire a manager to oversee some of his duties so he could reduce stress. We ran the numbers, and guess what? He decided he wasn't as stressed out as he thought he was. He didn't hire a manager, because the budget told him he couldn't make the overhead to pay for one. In the end, he really did save himself some stress: imagine if he'd hired someone without figuring it into the budget. He could have found himself deep in the red. Talk about stressful!

Budgeting will stop you from making sporadic decisions that could be costly down the road. You can also have fun with it when that pesky advertising salesman comes and wants you to advertise in the Yellow Book. You can just say, "That's just not in my budget for next year." It gives you that "I'm in control" feeling, because you really are in control, to a point.

It's important to not treat your budget as if it's set in stone, but instead to think of it as a living document. Here's what I mean: Imagine that your next year's budget is done. January starts with a bang! Your numbers are in and they're tracking with your budget, so you're pretty excited. Then toward the end of February, things drop off. When you input the numbers into your budget, you're down by around 10%. That means your income fell by 10%, but your expenses remain the same. But because you're working from a live budget, there's no need to panic. All you need to do is cut your expenses and adjust your budget for March to offset the loss. Sure, some costs are fixed, but many are variable and those are the ones you change. That budget is your buffer against many of the unexpected ups and downs of doing business.

When you're running a live budget you spend the money on paper before you actually spend the money!

From now on, if you get the fever to buy a new tool or pickup truck, you'll do what most responsible business owners with a live budget do. You'll enter the cost of the new tool or pickup into the budget and see before you spend the money how it will affect your income.

Now that you have a budget, you will get used to thinking of percentages very differently. Just a 1% increase in overhead can cost you way more than you think. That pickup truck is a good example. Say it has a price tag of $35,000 and you worked a genius deal, a 60-month loan at 4% interest with no money down. That comes out to a payment of approximately $644 a month. If your monthly budget projects $50,000 in total sales, your truck payment would represent about 1.25% of the budget. That means you have to increase every sale you make by 1.25% to cover that payment. That might not sound like a lot, but let's do the math: If your sales increase to $600K a year, your overhead increase is $7,735 a year for five years.

You might think, *That's not too bad.* But wait! Maybe you'll discover other unexpected needs next year, like new computer software, another van, or a new GPS tracking system. Pretty soon your overhead increases from 1.25% to 5%, or $30,000 a year! Now your budget has no wiggle room. Then comes the day when you're on a sales call and you bid the job at $7,500 but lose it to a competitor who bid at $7,000. You couldn't go that low because you would have missed your profit margin. Your overhead just priced you out of the market! Remember, a 1% increase can lead to lost jobs, which means lost revenue.

The best way to look at any type of purchase is this way: An asset will put money into your bank account and a liability will take it out.

Yes, borrowing money can be a good thing if it puts money in your bank account and doesn't put you at high risk of taking more money out than it puts in. But no, a brand new truck does not make you money. You can purchase a five-year-old truck for a third the cost and it will still do the same things the new one will. And if you buy the used truck, now you can budget to save a certain amount each month for a replacement truck. The big difference is you're putting the money back in your checkbook and not paying it out in payments. So if a lean month comes along, you can easily offset that payment and nobody gets hurt.

Step Eleven: Cash Flow. In business, cash is king! But profit and cash flow are not the same thing. If you stop making profits you can make budget adjustments, but if you run out of cash you're broke. When you respect the critical importance of cash flow, you no longer need to dread that old saying: "There is always more month than money."

You might be busier than ever and running a 10% net profit, but if the number in your accounts payable column is higher than the balance in your checkbook, you have no cash flow. You might think, "But I have it in accounts receivable!" That doesn't matter. If it's not in your checkbook, you're dead in the water. And what happens if the payment doesn't come in? Then you can't pay the accounts payable, you can't order parts, you can't pay your employees (if you have them), because your account is on hold. You are dead in the water.

Some people reach out for a line of credit. But that line can turn into a noose. It might work in the short term, but in the long term you'll be paying interest, which is costing you yet more money.

If you want to stay out of trouble, here's a simple way to look at cash flow: always have enough cash on hand to pay all your expenses for 90 days, without borrowing, in case money stops coming in. So, if your monthly expenditures are $10K a month, you need to have $30K of cash on hand.

Having a written business plan, with a live budgeting system at its heart, can only increase your chances of success. Not having one definitely increases your chance of failure. It's this simple: if you don't know where you're going, how will you know how to get there? If you've never written a business plan, or especially a budget, before, I recommend having a coach or mentor help you, someone who has already been where you are and who knows the way to where you want to go.

Chapter 3

You Won't Grow Unless You Market

*People are in such a hurry to launch their product or
business that they seldom look at marketing from a bird's
eye view and they don't create a systematic plan.*
– Dave Ramsey

One major pitfall small business owners face is how easy
it becomes to spend the majority of their time working
in their business instead of working *on* their business. When
all you're doing is rushing from call to call, to-do list to to-do
list, emergency to emergency, then your business doesn't
grow. And if your business is not growing, then it's probably
going backwards. Many small business owners who find
themselves in this situation will panic and look for a quick fix
to increase sales or cash flow. They'll look at different marketing ideas, trying to guess which one will be the quickest way
to bring in new business.

Marketing today can be very challenging because consumers are using the Internet to educate themselves about
products. Advertising through the newspaper, Yellow Pages,
or direct mail can be effective if done properly. But most
marketing today is not done properly and therefore produces
minimal results, regardless of the venue.

Does that mean marketing is not worth it? On the contrary. Effective marketing is one of your first opportunities to connect with customers and set the stage for successful sales. A fully functional marketing system that complements your sales system is essential to building a strong foundation for profit. Although this chapter will refer to marketing strategies for the home performance industry, you can effectively use these strategies for plumbing, electrical, or any in-home service business.

If you've already learned all the fundamentals of building science in home performance contracting (HPC), then you're ready to take the next step: learning to market your business. I've seen firsthand what happens when contractors go through all the training classes on building science only to fail when they try to market their business. Some advertise, but find out it doesn't work very well. Others sell tests, but have little success making a sale off the testing. I'm not here to teach you more about building science. Rather, I'm going to teach you how to successfully sell what you already have to offer in that arena, through effective marketing techniques.

The What, Who, and Why of Marketing

To lay our groundwork, let's run through the basic process of home performance contracting, better known by its hallmark test: blower door testing. This test was developed by scientists from the Department of Energy. They found that by testing a home with a blower door they could find all the hidden leaks in a home, leaks that can cause uncomfortable rooms or homes, health or safety issues, high energy bills, and other problems. For years, the solution to those leaks has been an array of products such as filters, UV lights, or zone systems. Don't get me wrong, those products are helpful, but they're only part of the solution.

The house is a system that we can look at as a tripod, with the equipment as one leg; the duct system as another leg; and the walls of the home, called the envelope, as the third leg. They all work together. That system, and your expertise in understanding it, is what you need to market. So how do you market that? Effective marketing and effective sales calls work hand-in-hand. To be successful at both, it's important to start with the beginning fundamentals and processes of your business.

Even if you're new at sales, you probably already understand the baby steps of a sales presentation. Most progressive salespeople have attended many sales training classes and have read multiple books, looking for better ways to increase leads. That's great. But you need to back up a minute. First of all, you need to define exactly what kind of results you want from your marketing.

Remember: marketing comes first, sales comes second. The difference between *marketing* and *sales* can be confusing. Many contractors spend thousands of dollars on marketing systems and programs, only to become frustrated when they achieve little or no result, especially in HPC. I believe that's partly because they're still thinking of marketing as part of sales.

Marketing: the action of promoting and selling products or services.

Sales: the transfer of goods or services for money.

Marketing is what puts you and your product or service in the customer's mind, and the *sale* is what closes the transaction. The first steps of marketing should be based on three fundamental questions. If you're not asking yourself these three questions every time you start a marketing campaign, your chance of railroading your own marketing efforts is really high.

1) What are you marketing?

2) Who are you marketing to?

3) Why are you marketing?

Let's answer each of those questions, one at a time. When you work in HPC, your answer to question number 1, *What are you marketing?* could cover a broad spectrum. That's especially true when you look at the whole house and all the opportunities it presents from a selling standpoint.

According to the Department of Energy: 9 out of 10 homes have indoor air quality problems! That is over 90% of your customers!

You can simplify your answer to the "What" question, if you focus on the needs of the client. In terms of client needs, you can put what you're marketing into four categories:

What Are You Marketing?

1) Comfort

2) Health

3) Safety

4) Energy

Comfort is by far the biggest concern your customers are experiencing. That's partly because today's consumers spend a high percentage of their time indoors.

Health is a concern all consumers have, though they may not be fully aware of how much their home affects their health. Today's customers are more conscious and conscientious about their families' health than ever before. Allergies and asthma are on the rise, and the home has a huge impact on how people experience those problems.

Safety is very important in the home, since people spend most of their time there. For HPC business owners this involves such products as carbon monoxide detectors and smoke detectors.

Energy is something homeowners think about whenever they're in the market for home improvements, primarily because of the cost of energy use. Today's consumers are interested in green options, not only because they can save money over time, but also because many people are concerned about the environment.

The above four marketing items represent points of connection you need to make with your customer. Focusing on those four needs will help you understand the focal point of what you're marketing. Knowing that you're marketing comfort, health, safety, and energy will differentiate your company from other companies, who are typically marketing product only.

Most consumers don't automatically understand an *energy audit* or a *blower door test*. Trying to sell those ideas will have very little effect on most people.

People don't buy on information,
they buy on emotion!

Let's look at question 2: *Whom are you marketing to?* Some marketing experts would put the question this way: Whom are you *targeting?* However you put it, the answer is simple: *homeowners.* But it can help to focus your marketing strategy if you're more specific. So let's answer it this way: *you are marketing to existing clients, new clients, and anyone you come in contact with who owns a home.* Remember, more than 90% of them have issues with their home! That number means home performance opens a huge window of opportunity for you.

If you think about *who* you're marketing to in terms of homeowners (90% of whom have issues with their homes) and if you think about *what* you're marketing in terms of comfort, health, safety, and energy—then you can create a whole new model for success. No longer will weather be the driving force that decides if your sales department will be busy. No longer will it be difficult to sell more products or services to a client with a two-year-old air conditioner or furnace. With this switch in approach, your market potential just quadrupled, and your customer base just multiplied tenfold!

Every client is now yours to lose.

I just showed you that 90% of homes have indoor air quality problems. You have been trained to find and solve their problems. Most of your competition does not know how to market to this bonanza. So you own the market place and if you lose the sales call it's your fault! Ouch.

It's time to stop worrying about your competitors, and instead let them worry about you! Believe me, they will. When I started using this marketing approach, some of my competitors began talking about me, and I loved it. They were advertising for me, at no charge! If you market this way, your clients will become your biggest advertisers, also free of charge. They'll advertise your business to all their friends and neighbors. Why will they do that? Because you'll no longer be selling them Band-Aids: quick fixes that only temporarily cover the underlying problems that are making their homes uncomfortable, unhealthy, or expensive to cool and heat. Instead, you'll actually be solving their problems in a comprehensive, long-term way.

Now that you know who to market to, let's move to question 3: *Why are you marketing?* The answer isn't as obvious as you might think. I've heard contractors answer the question this way, "I want to be known as the best heating contractor in town!" or "I want people to know we do the best service and installs in the area."

"That's great," I tell them, "but how are you going to do that when you're advertising someone else's product? Don't you think that you're making them known and not you?"

You might think that's not *you*, that you never advertise for your competitors, because you never mention them by name. But believe me, you're definitely advertising for them

49

if you're selling the same brand they are, the same way they are. They too sell themselves as the best heating contractor in town, offering the same services and products, for the same reasons.

Just look at your website. Does it say things like this?

- **We offer 24-hour service.**
- **Our employees are drug free.**
- **We are licensed, bonded and insured.**
- **We guarantee our work.**
- **We have the best products to offer.**
- **Ask us about our maintenance program, which can save you 15%.**

Now look at your competitor's website. Guess what? They say pretty much the same thing! Even if they're not actually the same as you, they advertise as if they are. My point: the above list of reasons is not *why* you are marketing. So what *is* the answer?

You're marketing because you want to own the market! You want to grow your business! You want to dominate your competitors every day of the year!

If you don't know why, you're wasting good money and time.

A Call to Action

One of the fundamentals of marketing is giving clients a *call to action*. You need to give them a reason to call you. How many reasons should you give them? If you know all their needs, then *all* those needs should all be reasons. You know they have comfort problems, you know they have health issues, you know there are safety issues that they would be concerned about if only they knew about them, and you know there are energy-saving potentials that they're not yet aware of.

The big mystery is you don't know which reason will trigger them to take action. You don't know which reason will make them pick up the phone and call you. So don't just give them one reason, give them a lot of reasons. And you need to target all those reasons with a focused marketing plan in which every part works together as a single whole, with a consistent message from start to finish.

You now know the four fundamental focal points of what you're marketing: comfort, health, safety, and energy. But how do you market those things? Your marketing campaign must arouse your potential customers' curiosity enough so they'll listen to what you're saying. If you make it clear that you have solutions to their problems, you won't have to sell them. Instead, they'll take baby steps toward you so they can find out more about those solutions.

Remember, whatever you do, your marketing materials need a call to action. That is, you must include an invitation for consumers to take a definite step that brings them into your sphere so they can find out more.

Example of a Marketing Promotion
HOMEOWNERS:

- **Are you experiencing uncomfortable rooms in your home?**
- **Do you suffer from allergies or asthma?**

- **Does anyone in your household suffer frequent headaches or flu-like symptoms?**
- **Are your energy bills going through the roof?**
- **You don't have to live with these problems any longer. Go to www.mybusiness.com to get a FREE report and watch a FREE video on how you can find the solutions. Or e-mail me@mycompany.com or call 1-800-000-000 today!**

The above marketing promotion includes three important components:

1) It asks *four probing questions* to uncover your potential clients' greatest needs, giving them four reasons to look at what you're offering.

2) It includes two *offers* of free information, so they can educate themselves on the needs they have, some of which they might not yet be aware of.

3) It includes two options for what they can do to receive the free information. Those are the *call to action*.

You might be thinking, "But everyone offers free stuff to entice people to buy from them." I agree. The Internet is overloaded with offers of free stuff. But that's not exactly what you're doing. *What you're giving away free is education.* There's no trick here. You're offering to educate your potential clients with real information, and you're also offering to educate them about why they're better off calling you rather than your competitor.

Remember, nothing is really free. Even if you're not asking for money, you are asking your potential customers to make an effort: to find out more, to provide contact information, or to contact you. But you're not forcing it on them. You're leaving it up to them. If they do take steps to find out more, you're prepared to reward them for their trouble with educational information.

This is a give-and-take scenario. If your potential client is not willing to give an e-mail address to receive a *free* report, is he or she really ready to buy from you? Probably not, but that's good to know. It allows you to focus on those clients who *are* ready to take the next step.

I can't stress enough how important it is for your free report to be a real piece of education, not propaganda for some sales gimmick. If you put a report together that tries to obligate your prospects to buy something, I guarantee you it will fail. A free report that addresses their needs must be legitimately educational and they should be able to verify the information via a third party expert. Having third-party verification will give credibility to the solutions you offer. That credibility will increase the closing ratio on the sales calls you make when these prospects are ready to buy.

Example of a Section in a Free Report

- **Are you experiencing high energy bills?**

- **Did you know that, according to the U.S. Department of Energy, a typical duct system loses 25% to 40% of the heating or cooling energy put out by your central furnace, heat pump, or air conditioner?**

- **The good news is that there are solutions to reduce your high energy bills!**

- **Call ABC Heating and Cooling to find out how you can avoid paying high energy bills and start saving money today! Call 000-000-000**

Every element of your marketing plan must include a call to action. One critical thing about making any call to action: you have to be ready with an answer for each one, and you have to follow through all the way to closing the sale. This is a call and response. Each step must include a plan for both: what action you're going to ask the customer to make to bring him a step closer to you; and what information, service, or product you're going to provide for him in return. Every step must be in place in order for a marketing plan to work. You need to create a process for applying your plan, and that process has to be the same throughout the company. If your plan is not thorough and consistent, it won't work.

Here's what I mean: Say that you or your marketing department uses marketing materials similar to the examples above, whether via the Internet, e-mail, snail mail, or flyers. Now suppose that you never set up an internal process for how to react when potential clients provide an e-mail address, watch a video, or call your number. If you're not ready with a specific response that keeps them engaged, you're going to lose them. For example, if they go see the video but there's no opportunity to contact you, you'll lose them, or if they call and nobody knows exactly what to say to them, they'll detect the awkwardness on the phone. That awkward moment will make your business seem unprepared and unprofessional, which could turn them away for good. You have to think this through from beginning to end, with prepared responses and policies for each move the customer makes in response to each call to action.

There's a lot to think about and do before you set this in motion. The good news is that once you do set it in motion, your marketing piece will quickly become a well-oiled machine that runs on its own momentum. Here are a few things to put on your checklist for a marketing campaign:

All Parts of Your Marketing Must Work

1) When you post website links, always test the links to ensure they're working before you send anything live.

2) Create a tracking system to tell you how your leads come in, so you'll know which parts of your campaign are working and which aren't.

3) Your customer service representatives and/or call center must be trained on how to process calls.

4) Your sales department needs detailed instructions on how they'll execute the process of completing their part of the response to your marketing campaign. They need to know the procedure from initial sales call to closing.

Rebates and Discounts Won't Set You Apart

Marketing instant rebates or discounts only gives your competitors time to offer the same promotions so they can take your clients away. It also opens the playing field, making you just another one of many bidders who will become a victim of price-motivated sales.

Rebates and discounts were once an effective method of marketing. In fact they can still be helpful for selling products such as TVs, appliances, and cars. But for your business, rebates and discounts are not strong selling points. They should only be used as icing on the cake when wrapping up a sales call. But they are *not* the way to make your business stand out from the crowd. You have to think more big-picture than that.

In your new approach to marketing, each call to action leads the client one step closer to the close of a sale. You don't get babies to take their first steps by pressuring them. You get them excited about the rewards waiting for them each step of the way. Not that you should treat a customer like a baby, but you get the idea. Remember, if you want to dominate your market, you must think in terms of cause and effect: For every action, you're seeking a reaction.

Although you don't want to be pushy, you do need to be assertive. This isn't about forcing them to action, but it is about calling them to action. You have nothing to gain by being shy about that call. If you don't tell customers what action they need to take to receive the value you have to offer, then how will they know what to do? If you don't include a call to action, you'll have to work twice as hard to land that customer. Tell clients what they need, that you can give it to them, and that if they'll do A, B, or C, you'll make sure they receive X, Y, Z in return. Make sure they know what you want them to do so they can receive what you have to offer.

You have to own the sales call, and the only way to own it is if you dominate the call from beginning to end. That only happens if you set the correct foundation for your relationship with clients long before you meet them. Otherwise, you'll be stuck in reaction mode. That means you'll likely continue reacting to overcome price. That puts you in an awkward position in which the competition dominates the sales call, when they're not even in the room!

Referrals and the Internet

I still believe the best advertising comes from referrals. But in today's market, referral clients will still check their friends' recommendations online, through company websites, referral sites, and social media. In fact, 90% of consumers research local products and services online. So any effective marketing campaign must take advantage of both referrals *and* the Internet.

You may think it's enough to simply have a web presence, but that's not enough unless you've completely thought through the message your website is conveying to customers. Many websites today are still stuck on selling, on telling customers to buy, buy, buy! But today's effective websites need to be about *educating* customers, not selling to them. Sure, your goal is to sell, but *your customers' goal* is to learn more so they can improve their lives. They already know you're in business to make money, but what do you have to offer *them*? That's what your website needs to be about.

"People love to buy, but hate to be sold."
— Jeffrey Gitomer

The three marketing questions I asked you earlier apply to your website, too. Before you set up your site, you must ask yourself: *what are you marketing, who are you marketing to, and why are you marketing?* Your marketing piece needs to be consistent on your website. It must be in sync with everything else you do to reach out to your customers.

Any calls to action that you give people outside of your webpage would be even more effective if they ultimately led to your website. And your website, too, must include calls to action. In return for every call to action, you must offer value. Your website should be full of value. In other words, your customers should feel better off after they visit your site, even if they haven't bought anything yet.

Education is the key to attracting customers.

One great way to educate your customers is by featuring educational videos on your website. Third-party educational videos are very powerful for getting customers to make a phone call to learn more. Free reports are also a great way to demonstrate to customers that you understand their problems, that you also know about problems they might not be aware of, and that you have real solutions for all of them.

The key to using free reports is to have an opt-in page, which requires your potential customer to give a name and e-mail address. The opt-in page is a great timesaver for you too, because it gives you an indicator that a client is truly interested. That way you don't waste time chasing down people who will be annoyed by what they perceive as high-pressure sales tactics.

According to a study from American Home Comfort: *Seventy-eight percent of your customers discuss their home comfort with an average of 5.1 people.* That's good news for companies who clearly address the concerns of their customers. But it's bad news for those who ignore customer concerns because they're so focused on up-selling tactics. Even if you are paying attention to customer concerns, if you're not getting that message across it could be detrimental to the growth of your business. Marketing is the way to get your message across: a message that says you care enough about your customers to serve and educate them before they've ever given you a dime.

Chapter 4

Educating Customers is the Key To Sales

If you work just for money, you'll never make it,
but if you love what you're doing and you always
put the customer first, success will be yours.
– Ray Krock

Are all heating, cooling, plumbing, and electrical contractors alike? Of course they're not. But the only way you can usually tell that is if you look deep. I mean really deep. That's because most contractors not only offer the same products and services, but also advertise those products in the same ways, in the same places, to the same demographics. Even when you call them on the phone, most give you the same sorts of product-based sales pitches. Their service seems to be something they expect you to take on faith.

But let's look at this process through your customer's eyes. Sorry, but this may be an embarrassing revelation for you.

Over the past year I've talked to heating contractors, plumbing contractors, electrical contractors, home remodeling contractors, and many other owners of small and large service-based companies. And most of them had the *exact same* problems.

Here are the most common problems they report:

- **The profit has gone out of the job.**
- **Price is what is selling the project.**
- **The phone is not ringing, even in extreme weather.**
- **I can't keep my technicians busy in the off-season.**
- **Marketing is not working.**

I was a heating & plumbing contractor for more than 20 years, and I'll admit I had similar problems. That is, until I did some digging. First, I looked at what my competition was doing. They were experiencing the same problems. That led me to believe that we must all be making the same mistakes. In that case, it made sense to me to put myself in the shoes of customers and try to figure out what might cause so many of them to make decisions that were causing all of us contractors to pull our hair out. In that spirit, I came up with three simple, but significant, questions:

1) **Why would customers hire me over the competition?**
2) **What was separating me from my competitors?**
3) **Why would customers want to pay more for my services?**

I thought about what I do whenever I'm a customer in the market for a product or service. As a customer, I look for three things: 1) good service, 2) a quality product, and 3) a fair price. It stands to reason that that's what my customers want, too. Okay, so how do most customers find those three things?

When consumers are in the market to buy, they'll most likely start with the most convenient path, which today means researching to find the best products out there, and to see who will give them the best service for a fair price. Let's consider how they do this shopping. Some talk with friends, neighbors, and coworkers they know and trust. Absent a strong recommendation from someone who lives nearby, many go to the Internet to find a few potential contractors who might fill their needs. Typically they'll call the first three or four they find online who look reasonable. And look at most of the contractors on the web: for the most part, their pitches talk about their products and discounted services. Blah, blah, blah. It all looks the same.

At this point, if the customer doesn't see the difference between each contractor he'll base the final decision on price. Home repairs tend to be big investments, and not the type most people want to spend a lot of money on. To them this is an annoying matter of necessity, even if it is the heart of their home. It's not like buying a house or car, where they're considering how much they'll enjoy looking at, living in, or driving around with something new. They just want their problem to go away with as little trouble or outlay as possible.

You can't blame them, can you? I do the same thing when it comes to a big purchase. I want to spend my hard-earned money on the best system at the lowest price.

So, now that we're settling into your customers' shoes, let's look at what they see when they find you online. Perhaps your company offers:

- **24-hour service**
- **Our technicians are drug-free.**
- **We guarantee our work.**
- **Best product warranty in the industry**
- **Bonded, licensed, & insured**
- **In business for X years**

The list goes on and on, yet it all sounds like what most contractors are offering, doesn't it? So if the lists are all the same, the choice will likely come down to price.

The average closing ratio on HVAC sales is about 30% across the country. Some companies boast higher closings but they usually give up profit to attain a higher ratio, so their bottom line isn't vastly different from anyone else's, and sometimes may even be worse. If you and your competitors are all dueling over price, and you can only drop your price so low before you lose money, then how can you set yourself apart from the competition?

Set Your Business Apart

You know that you're an honest businessperson who wants what's best for your customer. You might also know of a few competitors who use dishonest, high-pressure tactics to get more business. But it's pretty hard to tell your prospects that your competitor sucks and that they should pay you more, even though you both offer the same thing. I know the feeling. I've often wanted to tell a customer that he was making a poor choice by going with another contractor. But trying to make a sale by downgrading someone else can backfire by making you seem petty and greedy, which makes you appear even less trustworthy to potential clients. It just comes across as so much desperation and sour grapes.

And who was I to bad-mouth my competitors if they were able to make the sale and I wasn't? Who was it that got me into this dilemma in the first place? I was the one who failed to convince the customer of what I had to offer. I wasn't doing a very good job of selling long-term quality and service versus short-term price. Oh, I *thought* I was. But my desperation was showing, and so was my lack of understanding about how to sell. I was still telling them everything they needed to know about the product, and expecting that my commitment to honest, quality service would be obvious. "I offer the best service money can buy!" Yeah, yeah. That's what everyone else was saying too.

It really is no wonder why so many customers make decisions based on price alone. But I discovered that some contractors really can and do sell for a higher price. How do they do it? I found out how. It's all about a sales process that I still use on a daily basis, as do many consistently successful salespeople. Not until I was introduced to this simple approach of system selling did my closing ratios soar and my net profit margins climb into the double digits. Soon I began hearing the word going around town from my competition: "He was higher priced and he still was awarded the job." This was music to my ears. And it worked again and again.

My system boils down to one word: **education**.

You do not have to spend thousands of dollars every month, advertising for new customers. You do not have to keep offering value packs or discounts to get new customers to call you. You do not have to send out thousands of direct mailers, hoping for one response. You do not have to low-ball the competition. You do not have to starve during the slow season and hope to make it up in the busy season.

All you have to do is educate your customers.

To explain what I mean, let me first go back to the average closing ratio and consider the unexplored opportunity it represents. Let's say you have an average closing ratio of 30%. That means that for you to sell 30 jobs, you need to run 100 sales calls. For the sake of this example, let's say that an average replacement sale is around $4,500. That means that if you close 30 out of every 100 sales calls, you'll generate $135,000 in gross revenue. That might sound like a lot, but you know that in reality the cost of goods and overhead takes a huge bite out of that.

Now let's look at the flip side of that 30% closing ratio: for every 100 sales calls, 70 calls did not result in a sale. That represents a loss of $315,000 in sales revenues. Those are real numbers that have real costs.

I know that you can never hit a 100% closing ratio. But you know that even an increase of 10% in your closing ratio would bring you money worth talking about. In our sample scenario, that would mean at least $45,000 more in revenue!

Would you believe me if I told you that having both a higher closing ratio and higher profit margins at the same time is very possible? It is. You just need to develop your understanding of a little-known approach to sales calls. In this approach, your goal will not be merely to sell products and services, but instead to sell *education.*

If you want to stand apart from the competition, you need to give your customers more information than the competition. You must go beyond selling them the product that will solve their short-term emergency, and educate them about solutions to their long-term problems and needs. Most of them aren't even aware that those problems can be solved. Some of them aren't even aware that they have bigger problems than they called you about. If you can educate them, you can win them.

What Contractors Want

Over a period of one year, my company conducted a survey to find out the areas in which fellow contractors most wanted to learn solutions to their problems. We asked every contractor to rate, on a scale of 1 to 5, his interest in learning more about:

1. **Solutions to slow or money-losing periods caused by mild weather**

2. **Solutions to low-bid competitors who sell for less**

3. **How to prevent decent competitors from taking their jobs**

4. **New ways to increase average replacement job tickets and profit margins**

5. **Ways to increase net profit at the end of year**

6. **Ways to increase consumer satisfaction with new equipment or accessories**

7. **New ways to generate referrals and leads**

More than 85% of responders marked every question with a 5, meaning they were highly interested! You might think that would not be the case since the Internet is flooded with hundreds of sales and marketing programs that promise results, many of them available on inexpensive computer software. But, although some of those programs offer a few helpful ideas, HVAC, plumbing, and electrical contractors still aren't finding solutions to the seven problems above, which are the most important sales and marketing issues they face. Sure, it's a good idea to have software to help you track sales, get organized, and watch your trends, so you can catch problems before they become costly. But that's still not going to help you figure out how to increase sales revenue.

As I looked at contractors' responses to the seven items we proposed, I thought, "But this is what most sales and marketing systems promise to do. This is absolutely *nuts!*"

It turns out that contractors can solve all seven of the above problems with the one word I've given you, the one word that will lead you to consistently higher closing ratios: *education.*

What do I mean by education? I'm talking about educating the consumer through home-performance, question-based selling. Hold on a moment. It's not what you might think! I'm not talking about asking your usual questions about the customer's equipment or current emergency. I'm also not talking about asking leading, probing, or invasive questions that suggest a hard sell. In fact, most people don't like to be asked those kinds of questions—I sure don't! If you merely ask questions without knowing *how* to ask questions, you're going to get all the wrong answers, and again, you're going to miss the sale.

All too often, salespeople are too eager with their questions, using them as yet another tactic to push the client into something the client believes he needs. Let me repeat that last part: something the client *believes* he needs.

Let's say your technicians have been trained to up-sell on service calls. They've up-sold worn motors, filters, and so on. But did the customer really need that, or was that just part of your company's policy of pushing to get a bigger ticket? I don't doubt you're an honest person, but even the best intentioned among us can fall into this trap. Let me give you an example:

We'll say that your best technician just came back from one of the manufacturer's training classes on a brand new set-back thermostat. The manufacturer's representative has told him, "Every homeowner should have one," and bragged about how easy they were to up-sell. The rep has also fed him a list of facts about how this new product will save money for the homeowner. Your technician is so fired up he can hardly wait to go on his next service call. Upon completion of that next call, he spots that the homeowner has an older style thermostat, so he launches into a big spiel with the homeowner:

Technician: Sally, do you know that your existing thermostat is very old? Do you know most old thermostats are off by three or four degrees? The newer ones are much better. Let me tell you about this new set-back thermostat. It really can save you money and keep you more comfortable. You can set it up so it comes on in the morning and warms your house before you get up. When you leave for work it will turn back down for the day to save you money! We have a promotion

running on this for a short time. Your cost would be
_____. Would you like me to install one today?

Sally: Let me talk to my husband about it and we'll
let you know.

Does the above scenario sound familiar? More to the
point: does it sound canned and phony? I'll tell you one thing
I know for sure: the above pitch is not effective at all and can
be a real turnoff to your customer. Then why do so many
contractors tell their techs to up-sell products and parts?
They're looking for a way to increase their profit margin, of
course, and they can't figure out another way.

It could be that your technicians are so good at diagnosing
and solving problems that they spend very little time on each
call, which can cause a customer to say, "You sure charge a lot
for how little time you spent here. What's your hourly rate?"
Ironic, isn't it? When you're very good at what you do, that
can make it look easy, which can make the customer suspicious of your prices. If you have a customer who is happy with
your service, but believes your prices are too high, it's pretty
hard to ask for referrals. And as customer trust goes down
your business fails to grow, maybe even dwindles. What's a
contractor to do?

I was visiting a contractor who was looking into different
ways to increase revenue, so I asked him, "How does the process
go in your company when an emergency call comes in?" He
proceeded to tell me the process, which went something like
this:

"The call comes in and I send the technician out to the home
to find out what the problem is. The technician is supposed to

tell the customer what part has failed and then recommend that they apply the repair cost toward a new furnace or new air conditioner."

I asked, "What if the furnace is only four or five years old. Do you still try and sell new equipment?"

"Yes, we do."

I asked, "What about if the furnace is only two or three years old. Then what?"

"We'll probably fix it then."

That is nothing but box selling, with no thought at all about the customers and their real needs. It's no wonder contractors have a bad name for being high priced. This type of high-pressure sales might work for a while, but word soon gets around. In fact, with the increased education of today's consumers, this sort of sales tactic works even less than it used to. Today, many customers or prospects are getting two or three, or even four or five estimates before they make a decision. Contractors tell me that even longtime customers they have served for many years are getting more than one estimate these days. One contractor told me that even with existing clients he was only at a 45% closing ratio, because many of them switched to a lower priced company.

What changed?

People today are much savvier at looking up information. They're much more informed about the products and services they're buying. So if they know so much, how are you going to educate them? Didn't I say that educating customers was going to help you close more sales?

Yes and no.

Merely asking customers questions about what they think their problem is does not give you the opportunity to sell them something, nor does educating them about a product you're trying to push. In fact, if you go down that road you'll find yourself selling on price again. Today's clients can find all the product knowledge they want day or night. That's not the right knowledge to target.

I remember vividly trying to educate a customer about a furnace I was trying to sell. I had my product knowledge down to a science, at least in terms of what the manufacturer said the furnace could do. But when there was a pause in my pitch, the customer said, "That's exactly what my competitor's furnace did too, and he was $1,000 cheaper!" Needless to say, I did not get the job that day!

But it did make me stop and think, "What am I selling, a product or a service?"

You might be thinking that your business should be selling both those things as a package, a service that comes with a product. I beg to differ. Most contractors think they understand what it really takes to set their business apart from everyone else's. They'll say, "Service, of course." I remember visiting a business owner who had a very impressive business for over 20 years and claimed that the secret to his success was that he sold service over product.

He said, "Arne, we are in the solution business. We solve people's problems."

"Great!" I said. "Tell me how you do it."

"We find out our customers' problems and offer solutions."

I egged him on a little. "So, if I'm a customer who has dust issues, what's the solution?"

Without missing a beat, he said, "A media filter or UV light."

"Okay. If my problem is uncomfortable rooms, what's the solution?"

"We'd sell you a zone system."

I said, "So your solutions are products? What's separating you from your competitors? Isn't that what they're doing, too?"

His response was to circle back to where he started, "Well, you can look at it that way, but we are in the solution business."

That demonstrates the true definition of insanity right there: Do the same thing as everyone else and expect different results!

Don't get me wrong. There are still some successful box-sales people out there who deliver convincing high-pressure scare tactics: the good old "offer is only good till five p.m. today" pitch. And there are still some gullible customers who buy into that crap. But you might be surprised to know that these high-pressure box companies are finding out it's not so easy anymore. They, too, are looking for different ways to increase leads and sales because their pushy tactics are not getting them as many closings as they used to. I'm not surprised.

Most of today's customers don't just buy on trust. They verify before they buy, which I believe is smart. Many people like to search online for third-party reviews of a company's reputation before they'll hire them. Why risk being scammed when there are so many opportunities to double- and triple-check what you're getting into?

I remember one customer whom we had taken care of for years. She was an older widow who lived alone. One winter afternoon she called and asked if I knew an electrician who could wire her new furnace. When I asked her why she needed an electrician, she told me quite a story. She said she had received a letter in the mail saying that if her furnace was such-and-such an age she should get a new one, and that she could get one by investing as little as X amount of dollars. So she called the number on the letter and asked for a quote. She ended up being pressured into buying a new furnace even though there was nothing wrong with her old one. But the story didn't end there. When the contractor installed the new furnace, the wiring did not have a ground, so the workers told her she needed to hire an electrician to run a new wire. They took her money, and left her with no heat.

Unbelievable!

I ended up calling an electrician for her and making sure she had heat. Those guys who took the money and ran were definitely not in the solution business. If you say you're in the solution business, and if you want to succeed, you had better have real solutions to solve real problems, not Band-Aids.

The key to solving your customers' problems is education. That is, home performance, question-based selling.

Question-based selling has been around for a long time and is very effective, *but only if it's used properly*. Most of the time, the seller asks leading questions, already knowing the answer he or she is trying to get, and the customer feels that it's part of some sales scheme, even if it's not. Most of the time customers won't even give true answers, because their guards are up. They fear that if they say too much, they'll be trapped into buying something they're not sure they need.

If you ask a question about a customer's home, the ultimate answer you're seeking should be the answer to the question, "What's in it for the customer?" *not* "What's in it for me?" Contractors often rush to ask a set list of questions before they've really earned the respect of the customer. For those contractors, the agenda is "close this sale." The customer can smell that agenda from a mile off. Only when you make the effort to first earn the customer's respect, will you get answers to the questions the customer really needs to answer, the answers that will reveal what he really needs you to do for him. If you push your customers, you're going to get the wrong answers, leading to the wrong solutions. That sure isn't the way to be in the solution business.

Here's what I'm talking about: say you need a new washing machine because yours went out. So you head to a big box store to look at washing machines.

No more than a minute after you arrive, a salesperson comes up and says, "Can I help you find something?"

Isn't your immediate response typically, "No, we're just looking"?

Why do we say that? We definitely need a new washer, and we came in here to buy one, so why did we brush off the salesperson? Could it be that we did not want to hear some sales pitch? If that's the case, then why would we think someone would invite us to their home because they want to hear a sales pitch?

If you've had any kind of training in sales, you've probably been told many times to: first, have an introductory elevator pitch; second, establish credibility; third, uncover the customer's pain or need; fourth, show him the value; and finally, close the sale. Sound familiar?

Let's break down the way most people approach the above steps. Although they're the **right** steps, this is the **wrong** way to look at them:

Right Steps, Wrong Approach

Introduce Yourself – You tell the customers who you are, how long your company has been in business, how long you've been with the company, and your background.

Establish Credibility – You tell them the great service you have to offer. You tell them your company is licensed, bonded, and insured. You assure them your employees are drug free. You make sure they know you're a top-rated company.

Uncover Your Customer's Needs – You launch into a questionnaire about the customer's home:

What's the hottest room in the summertime?

What's the coldest room in the wintertime?

Do you have dust problems?

Are your utility bills high?

…Or an array of prepared questions.

Show The Value – You show your customer how the new equipment you're offering will solve the problems you've uncovered with your needs assessment.

Make the Sale – You write up a proposal based on what you discovered and go for the close. That's when the objections come out. So you try to overcome the objections. You think you're doing pretty well until the bombshell comes: "Your competitor is offering the same thing and it's $1,000 cheaper!"

I'm not saying that you don't need to do the above steps. You do need to educate the customer, you do need to ask questions, and you do need to uncover the customer's need so you can offer solutions. But let me give you a new way to look at the first thing you need to do:

You need to gain mindshare with your prospect. Or, as I like to put it: **You need to create curiosity to gain mindshare.** You need to gain trust by refraining from selling until you've really informed yourself and your customers about everything entailed in the entire system that is supposed to keep their home comfortable, healthy, safe, and efficient. This information is something you explore together. That's mindshare.

Asking the customers questions can't just be a way to sell a product, but instead a way to gain information about what the underlying problems are for their entire system. In turn, their answers must not be just a way to sell a product, but instead an opportunity for you to offer to test to find out where their problems are coming from. In turn, that test isn't just something else for you to sell, but instead an opportunity for you to offer the customer the most informed, complete solution possible. That's mindshare.

You're not just offering a product, like everyone else. You're offering to educate your customers so you can show them what's really going on throughout their home. That's mindshare.

They may have called you because their furnace is out, but even when their furnace is working their home comfort system probably has other problems. Some of those problems are things they're aware of, though they've probably assumed there are no solutions. Some of those problems are things they're not aware of, but would want to fix if they knew about them. Helping them find out the real problems and solutions that will make their home comfortable at a reasonable price, rather than just offering them another piece of equipment, is the start of setting your business apart.

Mindshare is the solution to higher closing ratios, higher profit margins, and happier customers. In Chapter 5, I'll explain to you why home performance-based selling is the best path to increasing the opportunity to truly educate your customer and gain mindshare. Then in Chapter 6, I'll explain to you the step-by-step sales system that will help you gain mindshare with your customers, and make more and better sales.

Chapter 5

Home Performance-Based Selling is the Key to Mindshare

It's always about mindshare, not market share.
– Ron Johnson

One of the most uphill battles for small businesses today is making enough money in sales to actually see a profit. My background is in sales, so I understand a lot about this.

My sales experience started at a very young age. When I was a boy, I sold newspapers. During high school, I worked the summers at a nursery where I did retail sales. For the past 24 years, my sales experience has been in heating, plumbing, and electrical. In that field, I've worked in every capacity, not just sales, but also managing day-to-day tasks, marketing, budget forecasting, goal setting, and customer relations. If you're just starting your contracting business, rest assured I've already done everything you're doing and more, the good, the bad, and the things you're still wondering about.

I've performed many seminars for homeowners on the whole-house approach to building science, educating my clients about why just purchasing a new piece of equipment may not solve their direct problems. Consumers today are on information overload via the Internet. They have access to every type of product you can imagine, especially home improvement products that provide heating, air conditioning, plumbing, and electrical. Do-it-yourself projects account for $910 million in home improvement products annually.

Not that many years ago, whenever a customer needed a new piece of equipment he would go to the Yellow Pages or the newspaper, call a few contractors, and ask two or three to come out to the home and give a free estimate. Today many homeowners start that process on the Internet. No longer do they just look up two or three names to call; they also research reviews of both the local contractors *and* the equipment they think they might need, all before they ever even pick up the phone. This has really changed the way an in-home salesperson must work.

People who work in retail sales typically sell merchandise, so it makes sense to focus on marketing and selling a brand or product. But in-home sales usually involve selling a combination of services and products, and that's a whole different animal. If you're doing in-home sales, then focusing on a brand or a product usually offers a very poor return on investment.

If you're a contractor who offers in-home sales, then consultative selling is a better approach. That means you're not just selling products or services; you're selling *solutions*. And that is a much different approach.

One of the biggest reasons in-home salespeople have a low closing ratio is because their marketing department advertises retail sales instead of in-home service sales. With that approach, the salesperson is doomed before he even starts. If that's your problem, the good news is, you can solve it.

Do you remember the reason you wanted to start your own business in the first place? You're probably an excellent technician, you love the features and benefits of the products you sell, you enjoy fixing things, and you feel good about being of service to people. Because you're good at all those things, you figure that you need to just do two things: sell a product, and offer great service. So you advertise that you offer great service, and figure there's nothing else you can do to prove that until after you've made the sale. That's why when you're trying to make a sale, you probably believe that all you have left to talk about is the product. You understand the technical aspects of the equipment, so you assume that's what your client wants to hear. That's not completely wrong: you do need to tell your clients about the features and benefits of the products that might help them. But that's only a very small part of the sale.

If your sales scripts are based on product selling, one of two things will happen: 1) you'll lose the sale because you're more expensive than the competition, or 2) you'll sell the job with a very low profit margin, to avoid losing the sale to the competition.

You can't win by focusing on selling products,
or on selling yourself.

Consumers today are asking one question: what's in it for me (WIIFM)? You need to be prepared to answer that question in a meaningful way that sets you apart. The way to do that is to give your customers information, not just information about you or a product you're selling—they've already researched all that. You need to give them information about their house's problems and how you can solve them. In short, your sales script needs to focus on offering your customers *education*.

Most sales scripts focus on product selling, or telling consumers all about your company: we're a drug-free company, all our technicians are certified, we're licensed and bonded, we offer 24-hour service, we've been in business X number of years. But the customer already learned all that from your website, as well as the websites of your competition. That information does *not* educate your customer. It's the same information your competition can give them. So you're still selling based on price.

Value building plays a big role in any sales call. There's a big difference between serving existing customers and attracting new customers. Existing customers have used your service for years. Trust has been established. You've serviced their equipment, and when you tell them it's not worth repairing they rely on your expertise about the best product to install. In this case, you're still making the sale based on product, but it doesn't hurt you much because you already have a relationship with this customer. In that instance, most of the time price doesn't matter.

The problem is you can't use those same tactics in a new customer sale, because the new customer doesn't know you yet. If all that person is learning about during your visit is the product, you're going to end up with a sale based on price only. In that scenario, most customers will award the project to the lowest bidder.

*Most customers go for the lowest bid for
one reason: You didn't give them a choice.*

The majority of salespeople are trained to sell products. When salespeople do that in home contracting, the result is low closing ratios. The salespeople don't lose the sales calls because the customer wanted to be cheap. They lose those calls because they messed up, by not giving the customer any other factors to consider besides price. The customer doesn't just want to know about the product you're trying to sell him, or that you're a nice guy. What the customer really needs is to understand everything you're going to do for him, and why he can trust you to do it right.

If you really think about it, the cheap customer is unlikely to call you in the first place. The really cheap customers are the ones who are buying online or from the big box stores and trying to do the job themselves.

Can You Do It?

Can anyone become a professional salesperson? Yes. If you believe it, you can do it. So is there a process to selling? Absolutely! It begins with honesty, integrity, and loyalty. If you cannot be honest and have integrity, you're not going to be a successful salesperson. Some people think that to sell, you have to sell out. That's not true. If you want to succeed at sales, you cannot sell anyone out: not yourself, and not your clients.

Many people have been brainwashed into buying the stereotypes about what you have to do to be a salesperson. For many people, the word "salesman" calls up an image of someone shady and dishonest. There's a reason for that: many salespeople have gone to the Dark Side, relying on dishonesty, high-pressure sales, gimmicks, and other methods that leave consumers feeling used. Why do people do it? As Obi Wan Kenobi told Luke Skywalker, the dark side is easier and faster. Underhanded, high-pressure tactics often give salespeople initial results in the short term. But those results dry up so quickly they don't know what hit them. The good side is not easier or faster, but it is stronger in the long run.

Having the proper training to be a visionary with clarity, integrity, competence, and comprehensive industry knowledge is essential to win over clients. But that's just a start. You're not selling products, or even yourself. You're selling knowledge and information. You're telling your customers everything they need to know about their problem and what you can do to help them solve it. You're educating them so that they feel ownership in the process. That not only creates trust, it empowers the client, and that's what closes sales.

Nothing can go forward in this world without sales. Everything we have, everything we do, we are selling or buying. Sales are an ongoing transfer of knowledge. It is all about overcoming objections before they come up. The best way to do that is to educate the customer.

New Standards Are Opportunities, Not Obstacles

Homeowners need their homes to be comfortable, healthy, safe, and energy efficient, yet 90% of them have a problem in one of those areas. You have solutions to those problems. They need something that a home performance contractor like you can provide, so why do so many contractors have a hard time closing sales?

Home performance contracting is a relatively new concept for heating and cooling contractors. But the newness of that field is not to blame. Many of these contractors were failing in their businesses long before they transitioned to the modern concept of home performance. Some contractors have been forward-thinking enough to implement some sort of testing, while others have implemented only that which is required by state or county code changes. But neither of those groups is doing very well as a whole. Very few look at home performance as a new opportunity, but rather as an inconvenience.

I have to chuckle when I hear contractors say things like, "Now the state wants me to test the duct system before I can get a permit! This sucks." If you really think about it, that state's new code just gave that contractor an opportunity to make $1,500 or more on each job! Figure it out: if you're doing four jobs a week, that's an add-on of $6,000 a week in revenue, at a 65% gross profit margin! Shoot, that sounds like an opportunity, doesn't it?

Others have looked into the new standards that are becoming the norm across the country, realized they would have to change the way they do business, and decided not to pursue it. Yet others are burning through lead after lead, trying to up-sell boxes to customers who are not ready to buy a new system, using high-pressure sales tactics or gimmicks to close sales. Many of that second type are trying to bypass new codes, telling the homeowner, "It will cost you X amount of dollars to test your ducts, or we could just install the new equipment without a permit, and you'll save money." Those sorts of contractors really have their heads stuck in the sand!

If you don't see the opportunity here, you're not looking hard enough. Remember, 80% of heating and cooling contractors say there's no profit left in the job, and more than 80% of them say they'd like to fill in the money gap during their off-seasons! I've had homeowners tell me that every year they need this or that part replaced because their furnace guy told them it was the weakest part of the system. Wow, really? Yet when guys like that are introduced to home performance contracting, many of them say something like, "I'm not doing testing; what does the insulation and duct leakage have to do with me?"

After a little bit of investigating, I've found that those are the kind of contractor who used to work for other contractors. One day they had an entrepreneurial seizure. Maybe they thought their boss was raking in all the money while they were doing all the work, or maybe they just wanted to be independent. They had a passion for fixing broken things, and they thought it would be enough to simply repair broken furnaces and air conditioners. They were pretty sure they could work a lot cheaper than their former company and make better money for themselves. They got into business without really understanding the business side of things, without even considering that it was something they might need to learn if they wanted to succeed.

That's the sort of contractor who is constantly working *in* his business instead of working *on* his business. These folks are trying to make up for the price wars by cranking out volume, only to fail miserably because they can't keep that up. Often they can't even cover their overhead. The new van they bought four years ago just clicked over 200,000 miles, and they're still making payments on it. When a motor or transmission goes out, they'll be in big trouble, because they have no money set aside for repairs or replacements. They're not planning ahead.

Some contractors are quick to jump into something new like home performance contracting because it involves new tools, which they think will make them new money! But if they haven't made a business plan that includes an effective sales process, pretty soon they're staring at a roomful of shiny tools that can do pretty much anything but make them money.

Contractors who have experienced that disappointment often blame the new concept: "This home performance gig just doesn't pay. What was I thinking?" Does this sound like you?

Some more progressive companies that do have business plans still don't understand how to generate consistent sales. They've implemented home performance contracting by chasing rebate programs offered through their local utility. Their thinking is, "Wow, look at all these leads we get! All these opportunities to sell more boxes!" Some succeed at this for a while, only to be disappointed when the rebate program ends. Then they're back to wondering how they're going to make it work by continuing to sell boxes, which yield low closing ratios and low profits. They've given up and gone back to what they know best, like 99% of the other contractors, going through the old insanity of doing the same thing over and over and expecting different results.

Some are just waiting for the next program, hoping to get a jumpstart on their competitors. Others are using their shiny new testing equipment as part of a reactive approach. When they install a new system and a customer is unhappy, they go back and test to see why the equipment is not performing like it should. They have it all backwards!

In a desperate bid to make the sale, many contractors end up offering testing for free, solutions for free, and even some repairs for free—all to keep their customers from going to someone else. Boy that sounds real profitable, doesn't it? You might think this is funny, but sadly it happens to be true.

Some people are so fearful of change that they'd rather stare at their small successes, and ignore the fact that in the big picture their business is on the ropes. I've heard with my own ears how a company had an awesome box sales person and didn't want to mess up his system, even though they had a warranty issue with his sales. They justified it by saying, "But he has a system that really works and brings in revenue!"

Home performance selling cannot be implemented halfway; you would do better never to start home testing, rather than commit to it only part way.

"But I Can't Afford It"

One of the biggest objections I hear from people afraid to jump into home performance testing is, "It's too expensive. I can't afford to start HPC in my business right now." Too expensive? Compared to what? A new truck or boat? All the equipment you've bought for your business so far that isn't getting you enough business? Sure, it might be too expensive if all you're doing is spending money on something that won't give you any return. But this is not just an outgoing expense. It is an investment that will pay you back pretty quickly, and then some.

The best way to look at an investment is to ask yourself one simple question: "What impact will it have on my business?" Understanding when to invest and when not to invest is key. I look at new expenditures in terms of liabilities versus assets. A liability will take money out of my checkbook every month, whereas an asset will put money in my checkbook every month. If an investment puts money in your checkbook, then it really isn't costing you anything at the end of the day. Shouldn't you be investing in your future?

But if you want to make a return on this investment, you do have to commit. If you try to stick to your old way of doing business, and just add a little home performance testing and service here and there, not only are you unlikely to be profitable, you also could end up seriously harming your customers. You risk earning a reputation for being unreliable. And that's definitely not going to grow your business.

If you're going into home performance contracting, you need the proper training on all aspects of the home. That's true even if you subcontract out some of the work. At my company, we sometimes hired subcontractors to do work where we did not have as much expertise, but we still had an in-depth understanding of not only what they were doing, but also how it would impact the home. This was critical to ensuring that our customers got what they paid for, which was critical to our reputation, which was critical to keeping our existing customers and gaining new ones.

You can't guess at any of this, no matter how much you think you understand about home systems. That can be downright dangerous. For example, changing a system by just sealing the ducts can change the pressures in the home, which could cause back-drafting of a natural vent appliance, which could lead to carbon monoxide poisoning in the home!

In a less dramatic example, sealing up a duct system and not balancing the system or sealing the other leaks in the home can increase dust problems. This time your customers are probably in no danger of dying, but the dust could make them unhealthy, and will definitely make them unhappy.

Do yourself and your customers a favor. Don't get into home performance contracting until you're ready to completely educate yourself first, before you try to educate your customer.

How You Make a Profit

There is a lot of confusion about how home performance can be a profitable business for a heating and cooling contractor or for a home remodeler. To understand that, let's first go back to your roots. You're a technician at heart. You've been trained to find failed parts in a system, tell the homeowner what you've found, tell him what it will cost to repair, and get authorization to do the work. That still works great for emergency work, because the customer is expecting to hear bad news. But if we apply this same approach to what we've learned about building science, it will come across as negative.

Consider this scenario: you're on an emergency service call. You inspect the home's duct system and you can see the telltale signs of ductwork leakage.

After you've looked everything over, you address the homeowner something like this: "Sally, I want to show you how leaky your duct system is." You show her. "See the dirt around the registers. You should really seal your ducts up. Would you like me to give you a price to fix this?"

If Sally is a considerate person, she might say, "Sure." So you put a price together. When she sees it she says, "Let me think about it and get back to you." Then you never hear from her again.

If Sally is a suspicious, aggressive person, she might even become defensive the moment she sees the price. Although she knows little about her duct system, why it's so important, or why it costs so much to fix it, she knows all about sleazy salespeople and she's sure you're one of them. She might ask why you're charging so much, or flat-out accuse you of trying to up-sell her. As soon as you go down this road of accusation, it can kill the sale.

Okay, if that's not the way to do the sale, then what is? In home performance-based selling, the optimal sales approach is systematic. You can't just wing this. Maybe you already have a scripted approach to sales, but that's not enough. It has to be the right script. Your company may be great at box sales, but that's not how you're going to make a profit. If your sales pitch is focused on products, or even on you as the product, you have to throw out the script. You have to know how to give people all the information they want about their problem and all the information that you know about how to solve it. You have to be able to answer every potential question or objection: not with defensiveness, not with assurances about how great you are or the product is, but with more information about the problem and the solution.

91

---

*You have to be prepared to educate every customer.
That means that, like any good teacher,
you have to have a lesson plan.*

Because consumers are more educated about products today, if you focus on the product you can end up on the defensive. You don't want to go to the call with that kind of disadvantage, finding yourself in a reactive mode instead of leading the sale. Even clients who have done business with you for years are *not* a sure thing. They may like you, but they're spending their hard-earned money on this equipment, and if they're not sure they're getting the best price, then they aren't going to let your relationship stop them from finding a better value elsewhere.

This has caused many salespeople to go back to their bosses and say, "We need to lower our price if we want to get the job!"

That's not the answer. The answer isn't to change the *price*. The answer is to change the *conversation*.

Home performance-based selling is one of the best ways to start branding your business, to build real value that builds mindshare with your customer. Building that mindshare with clients will clearly demonstrate to them why you are different from your competitors.

I remember talking to a very professional contractor who related a sales call he was on. The home was that of an existing client he knew fairly well. He went through his sales process, explaining the features and benefits of the equipment he was selling. His big advantage was that the manufacturer had a 10-year warranty on labor and parts. The homeowner really liked the warranty and said so. This customer had always been happy with all the previous service the contractor had provided. Nonetheless, the homeowner had already gotten some other bids, and said something to this effect: "I really would like to go with you, but your price is a lot higher than your competitor. I know their service isn't as good as yours, but I just can't see paying more for the same product." The homeowner even said he would like to have the competitor install the equipment but would still like to have our friend do the service work on it.

You see my point: the homeowner knew that our guy offered better service, he liked our guy, and he even liked our guy's product. The only thing that cost our guy the sale was the price. Do you blame the homeowner? I don't. He saw the value in this contractor's service, but since the sale was based on the product, why would he want to pay more for the same product? That contractor did not build mindshare with the customer.

Doesn't his story remind you of another industry? Price is also the deciding factor in auto sales. Dealers know this, so they advertise a vehicle at a very small margin over invoice and hope to sell an extended warranty to make any money. If you want to be in box sales, you can expect the same sort of results.

You may argue that you have a higher closing ratio with your existing customers and don't see this problem. But if we dug a little deeper into your sales, I'm confident we would see that your cold call or new customer sales ratio is very low, maybe 10%. Many contractors write these off as "price shoppers," but I'm pretty convinced that's not true. Price shoppers are not calling contractors. Price shoppers are the ones who buy equipment online and have some backyard guy install it for a few bucks on the side.

Price is not the deciding factor for most people. It's only a deciding factor if the salesperson doesn't find a clear way to make value supersede price. Research shows that this is how clients in our industry decide whom to contract:

How People Buy

- **Twenty percent buy based on price. (These are not your customers.)**

- **Thirty percent buy based on who they know and trust. (These are your customers.)**

- **Fifty percent will pay a higher price if they see the value, but if they don't see the value they'll buy from whoever offers a lower price. (These could become your customers!)**

That's right, *half* of your potential clients will make a choice based on value, if only you'll show it to them. If you don't show them any other value besides price, then price will be the only value difference they have on which to base their choice.

You might be tempted to think that even if you tried to sell based on value, you would never be able to compete with larger companies. But I can tell you for a fact that I've seen some big companies that have struggled as they've added home performance as part of their business. Smaller companies are starting up in their marketplace and giving them a run for their money. The reason I'm getting to know these bigger companies and their difficulties in making this transition is because they've contacted me to help them figure out how to change their sales systems. They know that home performance is here to stay.

Many businesses, big and small, are getting their personnel trained and certified in the building science of homes. These companies see the moneymaking opportunity in new energy, health, and safety regulations for homes. They're investing in the fact that homeowners are becoming educated about the new whole-home approach. Many have started the process of offering testing and solutions to homeowners across America. *These companies are taking customers that could be yours!* They're discovering customer problems you've overlooked because you haven't been asking the right questions. Below are some of the complaints customers have about their home systems, complaints that represent opportunities you're probably missing.

Problems Homeowners Are Complaining About

- **Asthma and allergies**
- **Uncomfortable rooms**
- **Dust issues, even after they've installed high-efficiency filters**
- **High energy bills, even after new equipment has been installed**

This is a fantastic time for you to get in on solving these problems, partly because this field is still relatively new, and partly because so many other companies aren't up to speed yet. Progressive contractors know they need to implement HPC into their businesses, but they're all having a harder time than they anticipated. Their biggest dilemma: how can we make it work with the sales system we worked so hard to implement and that served us so well in the past? No doubt that is a much bigger challenge to a large company than a small one, because they have to deal with ingrained corporate culture.

Big company or small, the hardest people to get to buy into this new approach are salespeople. That's because they've spent years selling products, rather than selling tests. Those tests provide homeowners with more of that thing I keep telling you is so important: education. Testing gives you a way to tell your homeowners more about what's causing the house problems they're having.

Think about it. What did you used to do if your client had uncomfortable rooms, high utility bills, humidity problems, or allergy problems caused by dust? Your solution was some product to solve the pain. Sometimes you got lucky and it worked. But not always. That's because for years there was no testing. In fact, for years, nobody even thought that something like a leaky duct system could trigger a child's asthma attacks. So the problems were not solved, and the consumers were not satisfied. They started to look to other products for help, such as portable air purifiers or humidifiers. But those were just Band-Aids that weren't addressing the underlying problem. Even before you knew about the whole-home approach, maybe you chuckled a little when you saw those sorts of products in your customer's home, thinking, "What a waste of money!"

Now we know better. Now we have more solutions to homeowner problems. And now I'm here to tell you there's another way to look at your customer's problems. My customer has a significant pain or need, and is willing to spend money to fix it. If I can identify the cause of the pain, and educate this customer about the solutions, I can make a sale.

Today's salespeople have no choice but to change, because of one simple factor: customers have changed. More than 90% of them are doing research online for local products and services! Those are your clients.

So, how can you be successful in home performance contracting? If you learn all you need to know, and pass that knowledge on, how can you *not* be successful?

It's a new era in the HVAC world, a rather exciting one! It does require change. Are you ready? Great, then let's move on to learning the step by step sales process that can make home performance contracting really work for you...

Chapter 6

Winning at Sale Number One

Most people think "selling" is the same as "talking."
But the most effective salespeople know that listening
is the most important part of their job.
– Roy Bartell

Whether you're a business owner or a salesperson, sales is how you make your money. So here's the big question that's the key to unlocking greater sales, if only you can answer it: what part of the sales process is it that makes a sale complete? Think about all the objections you've ever heard when trying to sell someone products and services. You may have even written a few of them down and come up with answers, so you'll be ready with an answer to overcome any objection the next time.

I've heard countless objections over the past 25-plus years:

- *We want to think about it.*

- *I need to talk to my husband (or wife) about this.*

- *We never make a decision without looking at all options.*

- *We don't have the money to do this right now.*

- *We're selling our home next year, so can you just fix it to get us by?*

- *You're a lot higher priced than your competitor.*

- *I can buy that at (name a box store) a lot cheaper and just have you install it.*

- *I really like what you have, but I want to sleep on it.*

We all know that the above excuses or delaying tactics are common when a client is not ready to buy. But what makes him ready to buy? No doubt, you've seen many processes for closing a sale. Most are similar, or at least give a similar message:

Steps to The Typical Sales Process

1. **Gain credibility.**

2. **Uncover needs.**

3. **Offer solutions.**

4. **Close the sale.**

But is that all there is to it?

I agree we do need to gain credibility, uncover needs, offer solutions, and ultimately close the sale. But people are not machines, and they don't want to be probed and pushed. Modern consumers want to be educated before they make a decision about where they'll buy their products and whom they'll hire to install them.

Let me take a moment to define in more detail the four steps outlined above. Then I can explain to you how to enhance those steps by *educating the customer*.

How the Typical Steps to Closing a Sale Work

Gain Credibility: If you want credibility, it helps to know the specific arena in which you hope to gain that credibility. Do you want to convince people that your company does the best work? That you have the most knowledge about solutions to your customers' problems? That your company is the most honest and reliable? Those are all a good start, so long as you understand exactly what you're selling. The only problem is, you're probably focused on gaining credibility for the wrong sale. Before I explain, let's look at the other three typical sales steps…

Uncover Needs: Before you start this part of the process, the question you need to answer for yourself is this: what are you trying to gain by uncovering the customers needs? No doubt you're looking for their pain or problem so you can come up with solutions that will help you close a sale. But why is it that, even though you always have solutions to answer your customers' needs, so many still won't commit to contracting you for the project? The answer is: both you and the customer are too focused on the product and the installation of that product, when what you really need is more *information* to solve the deeper home system issues that lie underneath the problems you're looking at.

Offer Solutions: Once you have uncovered your customers' needs, it seems a simple enough matter to offer solutions. After all, you know about products that can help. The thing is, so do they, because they've already learned about them online. So they're quick to agree with you, "Yup! That sounds like the right product, all right." But most of them still say, "We want to think about it," or they explain that someone else has already offered them a better deal. *Your solution failed to offer them something new that they didn't already know.*

Close the Sale: Sometimes this is a tall order, isn't it? If you're like I used to be, you probably often find yourself at the end of a sales call, and you know it's time to ask for the sale, but you're thinking, "Wait! I'm not ready. I don't get the feeling that this client sees the value yet." But you've run out of things to talk about, so you ask for the sale anyway, because you have to ask sometime and this is the end of the process you've been trained to follow. You're probably no longer all that surprised when a client says, "We need to talk about this and we'll let you know tomorrow." You probably write the client off at that point, knowing that tomorrow will never come.

I'm not saying your sales process is bad. You may have the picture-perfect process, which you've repeated to coworkers and friends who've agreed they would be sold on your pitch—if they were in the market for what you're selling. I used to go through the same four steps, and I had them down pat. I was great at it. There was only one problem: I was selling the *wrong thing.*

At the time, what always struck me was that it was clear most of the clients trusted me, that I had correctly identified their needs or problems, and that I had offered them the best possible product to solve their problem at a great price. But by the time I got to step four, I was still nowhere. If I executed every step perfectly, it seemed to me they should buy. So why didn't they?

When I couldn't stand being puzzled over that mystery anymore, I started to do research to see why so many clients never got off the dime. At first it made no sense to me: these customers called to get an estimate, so naturally I assumed they were in the market to buy, right? That was my mistake: *I assumed they had already made the decision to buy.*

The light bulb came on! I realized that for every sales call, I should be making two sales! I shouldn't only be solving the problem they called me about. I should also be solving the problem they did not tell me about: *that they needed more information because they weren't yet sold on the idea that they needed or wanted a solution.* If I could provide that, it would result in a much higher closing ratio.

Look at the average closing ratio today in heating and cooling in-home sales: it's less than 30%, with single-digit net profit. I don't know about you, but I believe it's a lot of work to run ten sales calls just so I can close three of them, all for single-digit net profits.

There are hundreds of sales processes out there and yet the average closing ratio is the same for almost all of them: less than 30%. Oh sure, there are a few companies that have higher closing ratios, but if you analyze them more closely, you'll find that their breakdown isn't as hot as it seems.

Take Tim, a very successful business owner who told me he was at a 60% closing ratio. I said, "Wow, that's great for box sales!" Then I asked Tim if he tracked where each sale came from, such as existing customers, referral leads, or cold calls. He said yes, and pulled out a spreadsheet detailing all of the calls his company runs. Upon evaluation, we discovered some very stunning results.

Yes, Tim was at 60% with existing customers, but with referrals he was at 22%, and with cold calls he was at 14%. Upon reflection, his results didn't look so hot anymore. A closing ratio of 60% might look pretty high at first glance, but not when you consider that number refers to *existing customers*. Those should be a slam-dunk, because they're people who have already done business with you. Existing customers and the people they refer to you should be hitting 80-90% closing ratio. And a 14% closing ratio on cold calls is costly, don't you think? What's worse, the average contractor isn't even doing as well as Tim:

Typical Closing Ratios for HVAC Sales Calls

Existing maintenance customers: 60% closing ratio

Referral customers: 60% closing ratio

New client cold calls: 10% closing ratio

But you can do so much better than that, if you'll remember that there are two sales to every one sales call. That's regardless of what you're selling, be it products or services. If your sales call doesn't close, most of the time that means that you didn't close sale number one. And you can't move to sale number two unless you've first closed sale number one.

What do I mean by two sales? Think of it this way: Christopher Columbus had to first sell the *idea* of a voyage to find the Indies, or *sale number one*, before he could sell the actual voyage to America, or sale number two.

The biggest assumption people in sales make today is that our clients are already sold on the idea that they need to buy this or that product or service. So, we start trying to sell them on reasons to buy from us, before we've sold them on the idea that they really need or want what we have to offer. This really changes the process of a sales call, doesn't it?

Before you can sell people a product or service, you must first sell them on the idea ***that they need to buy that product or service. That is sale number one.***

Sale number one is the most critical sale to close first, every time!

Let me give you an example closer to home: many people go shopping for a new refrigerator when the old one is still working. So although they're curious about what's out there, they're not yet sold on the idea that they need a new fridge. Let's say you're the salesperson who talks to them. Sale number one requires you to convince the customers that they need or want a new refrigerator. Sale number two is then convincing them that you are the person to buy it from.

The problem of jumping to the second sale before finishing the first one is an even bigger issue in service selling. When a client calls and asks to get a price on a new furnace or air conditioner, you might automatically assume they're going to buy a new furnace or air conditioner because they called for a price. But expressing interest in a price is not the same as being prepared to buy. First you have to convince people that they truly want or need a new furnace or air conditioner, and then you can move to convincing them that you're the one to buy it from. Otherwise you're putting the cart before the horse, and the horse is never going to budge.

I can tell you from experience; once I understood this concept of two-part sales, I began to succeed. When I spent more time on sale number one, the results were astounding. If I could not get a customer past sale number one, I would not even waste time trying to move to sale number two.

Sale number one is driven by this underlying question: "Are you in the market today to purchase services or products regardless of whom you buy from?"

If you start a call with your focus on sale number two—"Here's why you should buy from me"—you're wasting your time, plain and simple.

But wait, there's more!

Even though people today are much more informed thanks to the Internet, the information they get that way is often wrong. This is another opportunity for you to increase your sales potential, because it means the customer needs a lot more education from you. If you take the time and effort to educate him, this can really help you clinch sale number one and create the urgency to move to sale number two.

Are you ready to learn this more successful way of closing sales?

Sale Number One Starts with Curiosity

We initially started the sales process with the concept of gaining credibility. Although that's important to sales, it's not the first step when you're focused on sale number one. If you want to win sale number one, you need to back up, and instead start with curiosity!

Creating curiosity in your client is the first step in any sales call to start the process of sale number one.

Creating curiosity is the only way you can break through the fog of uncertainty or misinformation so that you can gain mindshare with a potential client. If you cannot gain mindshare, you cannot move one inch forward.

How many times have you been on a sales call, watching customers nod their heads in agreement? This might make you think they're really listening, when really they're just waiting for you to end your presentation and get to the price so they can see how it compares to the other estimates they've already received. The bottom line in that situation is that you never gained mindshare. That person was basing his decision on price right from the beginning. You let the nodding head convince you that he was listening to you talk about all the features and benefits of your products and services, and you failed to see it as a sign that he was not involved in the process. *You skipped to sale number two, and you lost.*

Or let's say you finish your presentation and tell the client the price, only to find out that she's just looking right now and will let you know when she decides to go forward. Wouldn't it have been nice to know that you hadn't yet closed sale number one, so you could have focused on that first? Now you've already pitched sale number two, and it's hard to dial that back.

But if you focus on the client's *curiosity*, that will uncover whether you're going to be able to close sale number one sooner rather than later.

Let me walk you through an example. Sally has called to ask for an estimate on a new air conditioner. The receptionist has taken the pertinent information:

- **Sally has a 20-year-old heating & cooling system**
- **Sally's system receives regular service from another company.**
- **Sally's house is 20 years old.**
- **Sally's home is two stories atop a basement.**

The receptionist makes an appointment with Sally, and as the time approaches you call Sally to let her know you're on your way. You park on the street, walk to the front door and knock. When a woman opens the door, you introduce yourself, confirm she's Sally, and hand her your business card.

You ask if you can come in, step in onto your drop cloth, and put on your booties. The next part of the conversation goes something like this:

> **You:** Sally, I understand you called in for an estimate on a new air conditioner.
>
> **Sally:** That's right.
>
> **You:** Do you mind if I ask what's prompting you to get an estimate on a new system?
>
> **Sally:** My husband said the one we have is on its way out, and he asked me to get a few bids.
>
> **You:** So your air conditioner is working right now?
>
> **Sally:** Oh yes. It works. We're just checking prices because we're hoping to get a new unit installed next year.

I wanted you to see this scenario, which is not the normal sales call, so you could get a sense for the way that working on sales number one first can help you save time. You now know that Sally is not buying an air conditioner today. Now that you know sales number one is a long way off, you don't need to waste time on sale number two. If you were to go for sale number two at this point, it would be all about price and the sale would simply go to the lowest bidder.

Instead, in the above scenario, your goal is to get another appointment with Sally and Bill. The way to do that is to create enough curiosity in Sally that she decides that her husband needs to be there when you present a proposal or estimate. Remember, you're not going to try to push her into making another appointment, which is likely to shut her down since she wasn't planning to buy anyway. Instead, in diplomatic and friendly fashion, you're going to give her so much good information that she wants to find out more, and wants her husband to be on hand to hear it. Here's an idea of what that might sound like:

> **You:** Sally, could you show me where the air conditioning equipment is? I'd like to run a free static test of your duct system. That's a sort of blood test for your house. This test will help me get a better understanding of your house and your home system.
>
> **Sally:** Sure, follow me.

This is where you're starting to separate yourself from your competitors, who do look at the equipment and take some measurements, but who don't do any testing. The reason for the test is twofold:

1) A test will tell you the static pressure of the existing duct system. It will tell you, for example, if the static pressure is 1.5 WC when it should be at .09 WC. Under that scenario, if you were to sell a new air conditioner for Sally and Bill, that would be bad news, because you'd also be buying all of Bill & Sally's problems! You see, an air conditioner isn't all they need if they want effective and efficient cooling.

2) A test gives you an opportunity to ask some deeper probing questions so you can uncover the real reasons for replacing the air conditioner.

Once you finish the test and have all the information you need, you can then pursue the following line of questions with Sally:

> **You:** Sally, do you mind if I ask you a couple of specifics about you and your home? Your answers may help me understand my test results.
>
> **Sally:** Oh. Okay. Like what? (Her tone tells you she wasn't expecting this, but that she's curious to find out what you're going to ask.)

People love to be asked about their lives, especially when their answers may help you tell them even more about their lives. And remember, their home is a big part of their lives. You have Sally's full attention and focus now, because she knows if she gives the wrong answers it could affect the outcome of what you're about to recommend. This is one way that you gain mindshare.

In the above scenario, many contractors would have simply given Sally a price and moved on, knowing they wouldn't be making a sale that day, or they would have dismissed her as a price shopper and not worth their effort.

Remember, Sally set the appointment because she is doing her due diligence as all homeowners do: she does want to get a price. She and her husband probably already did some research on products and features, and it's possible the only reason she called you is because you carry a product that has received good reviews. This does not mean you'll get the job.

Your opportunity here is to separate yourself from the rest of the bidders. If you were to start down the road with an elevator pitch about your business—"We've been in business for X number of years, we guarantee our service, yada yada yada…"—that's not what Sally called you for, and she's likely to close her mind to the rest of your pitch. That means no mindshare for you.

Similarly, if you start with "Sally, we really need Bill here before I can put a price together," she is also going to shut down on you. She's likely to say something to the effect of, "We're not doing anything till next year, and we know the price may go up by then anyway. Bill just wanted me to get a ballpark figure." You have just backed yourself into a corner; now you have no choice but to give her a price and leave.

Think for a moment about the important information Sally has given you. She called your company because both she and Bill think they need an air conditioner. She already admitted that their current air conditioner was on its way out. What does that really mean to them? Your goal is to find out the real reason they're interested in a new air conditioner. When you find that out, you'll be on common ground. And when you start asking Sally questions in that vein, she'll begin to realize that Bill needs to be part of the process. Here's an example of what that line of questions might sound like:

You: Sally, I understand that Bill said your air conditioner is on its way out. Could you explain a little bit about why you and Bill believe that?

Sally: I don't know. That's all Bill said. After all, it is 20 years old.

You: Sally, I understand. My job is to educate you so you can make the best decision when you do decide to purchase a new air conditioner. Often people make these decisions without getting all the facts, and that can lead to costly operating costs for years to come. Does this make sense? Understand, this sort of equipment alone won't solve many of the comfort issues, health issues, and energy costs we experience in our homes.

Sally, you watched me take the static test, that blood pressure test, of your existing system. Now, I can show you that your existing system is running over the manufacturer's specs. So by just putting a new unit in place of the old one, you might not solve the problems you were hoping to solve.

Did you know that the Department of Energy says that 20 to 40 percent of the energy we pay for is lost through duct leakage? So if you're looking for a more efficient air conditioner to help lower your utility bills, then installing a new unit could yield little to none of the savings you and Bill would like to see.

Or maybe you believe installing a new air conditioner will simply make you more comfortable. But if your duct system isn't working properly, a new unit won't help all that much with comfort either. Now I'm not saying you have these problems, Sally. I just want you and Bill to make an informed decision when it comes time to buy your new conditioner. Purchasing an air conditioner is a big decision, especially when you expect them to last for 15 to 20 years, wouldn't you agree?

Now that you have Sally really listening, here is the real meat of what you need to explain to her, to gain more mindshare:

You: Sally, when it comes to keeping your home atmosphere comfortable, it helps to think of your home as a system. One way to look at it is like a three-legged stool. Here are the three legs:

Leg Number 1 is the shell, or envelope, of your home: walls, ceilings, and windows.

Leg Number 2 is your central duct system, which moves air around to heat or cool your home.

Leg Number 3 is all the equipment installed in your home that impacts air quality and comfort, such as a furnace, air conditioner, filter, UV light, or humidifier.

You: All three of the system's legs have to work together if you want to maximize efficiency. If you'll help me understand how all three legs work in your home, I can then make the right recommendations on purchasing a new air conditioner. Does that all make sense to you, Sally?

When Sally agrees that what you're proposing does make sense, you have just gained credibility, as we talked about earlier. But the important thing to realize is what the purpose of gaining credibility is here: so you can start asking questions to uncover her need, not just the need she thought she had, but the need she really has. Once she agrees to continue, she has made it clear that she thinks you're competent to ask her deeper questions about the three legs.

The following are questions you now need to ask Sally to uncover her true needs:

Questions to Reveal the Customer's Needs:

1. In the summertime, which of your rooms are the warmest?

2. In the wintertime, which of your rooms are the coldest?

3. Does your furniture seem to get dusty again just a few days after cleaning?

4. Does your heating or cooling system ever run non-stop but still not keep you comfortable?

5. How important is it to you to save money on your energy bill?

6. Does anyone in your household suffer from asthma or allergies?

7. Does anyone in your household get frequent headaches, suffer flu-like symptoms, or feel tired all the time?

8. What is one thing in particular that you don't like about your current heating and cooling system?

It's important to let Sally talk about each one of the questions. Don't hurry her. When you ask the above questions,

Sally will see that you're very different from most contractors and will see value in furthering the conversation. You're gaining yet more mindshare.

Once Sally has answered all the above questions, the next step is to go back over the questions that revealed a potential problem and ask further probing questions. For example:

You: Sally, would you mind telling me a little more about the upstairs, which you said was the warmest area in the summer time?

Sally: (She explains when it's warmest, when she notices it most, how hot it gets, etc.)

Go through all the other questions Sally answered with a problem. Let her explain in her own words. Make sure to ask her if she feels that installing a new air conditioner will solve the issues she has described. Once you've gone through all the questions, Sally will no longer just be interested in an estimate. Now she'll be curious about what kinds of solutions might solve her issues. Once you know she's at that point, your next step is to ask her one of the most important questions you can ask during *sale one*:

"How important would it be to you to have Bill with us to hear about the solutions to the issues we've discussed? Do you think he might have some of his own questions he'd like to ask?"

At this point, the likelihood of Sally setting up another appointment when Bill can be present is very high. You've made excellent progress. When you started this call, Bill and Sally were asking about a new air conditioner, but were they ready to buy one? Not really. They just felt that their current unit was getting old, and as responsible people they wanted to get prices in advance of it breaking down, so they could replace it on their own time and not end up in an emergency call situation. They had not yet bought into the idea that they needed to change their system at all. Now you have Sally ready to be sold on a new idea: "Gee, we may have problems I never thought about; we may need more than just another air conditioner."

Sale Number Two

Let's assume that Sally convinced Bill to set up another appointment with you. Don't make the mistake of getting overzealous and assuming you've finished the sale. You've clinched sale number one. But that's not the sale that makes you the money.

The sale that makes you the money
is sale number two.

For that one, you're going to have to start over again and create curiosity with Bill. The good news is that Sally has already convinced him that you're a credible person who is worth listening to.

You will need to reiterate all your questions, now asking them of Bill. Make sure to let Sally be your ally here. As you refer to each question, recall what you discussed with Sally, give her a chance to chime in, and voice her concerns along with her.

Once you have reviewed all their needs, it's time to offer solutions. Remember, Bill and Sally will likely be looking for third-party verification on all the answers you give, so be fully prepared with your own third-party verification, which is readily available on the Internet—and it's free.

Offering Solutions to Clinch Sale Number Two

When I talk about offering customers solutions, I love using the analogy of the salesperson as a kind of doctor. When you have pain and you go to a doctor, he or she charges you money just to come in and ask for an opinion about your pain. Doctors do not offer prescriptions, or *solutions*, for free, do they? That's why one of the first steps you go through when you walk into the doctor's office is giving someone your insurance information, so the doctor has some assurance of payment.

When you go into the examination room, a nurse will then ask you some preliminary questions and do some preliminary tests to help uncover the pain you're experiencing. The nurse will write down your answers to the questions, weigh you, take your temperature, check your blood pressure, and such. Then you'll usually hear something like, "The doctor will be with you shortly."

For the next step, the doctor comes in and conducts more diagnostics, which may involve: asking more in-depth questions about the things you told the nurse; checking your lungs, heart, vision, and reflexes; or ordering a blood analysis, biopsy, MRI, or other tests. Once the doctor has enough information, he or she will attempt to diagnose the problem, and then prescribe something for your pain: sometimes it's some action you need to take, or surgery you need to undergo, but more often than not the doctor will prescribe medication.

Your final step in the process is typically to go to the pharmacy, fill the prescription, and start taking the medication.

If a doctor offered a prescription without doing any diagnostic tests, at least a physical exam, that would be malpractice! Yet that's not much different from what many HVAC contractors have been doing for years: offering solutions without testing.

HVAC contractors sell equipment assuming it will cure the problems their clients say they have. Sometimes it works, but often it doesn't solve the underlying problems the clients don't realize they have.

Needs Most Clients Don't Know They Have

- The Department of Energy says 9 out of 10 homes in America have indoor air problems. That's one reason asthma and allergy problems are on the rise.

- Over 50,000 people visit emergency rooms every year for low-level carbon monoxide poisoning.

- A leaky duct system can lose 20% to 40% of the energy that you paid for to heat and cool your home. (Dr. Max Sherman, Department of Energy, Lawrence Berkley National Lab)

With that in mind, let's go back to Sally and Bill. Let's say you've uncovered that the needs, or pains, that Bill and Sally have are uncomfortable rooms, dust, and high energy bills. Here's the solution you can offer them that most contractors won't:

> **You:** Bill, Sally, we've found that the best way to find solutions to the issues you're experiencing is by doing a home and duct performance test. It's like taking the blood pressure of the whole home. This test was invented by a scientist from the Department of Energy. This is how it works: we put an infiltrometer blower door in your doorway and take your home down to a negative pressure. It's like a 15-mile-an-hour wind pressing into four sides of your home at the same time.
>
> This test can help us find the cause of the issues you're experiencing in your home. We'll also measure your duct system to see where your energy is being wasted. We'll also find out why your upstairs is too warm in the summertime. We can also find out why you have so much dust.
>
> Now, we do charge for this test, but we offer it at a 100% risk-free guarantee. If after the test is complete you see no value, you don't have to pay us.

When you take the risk out with a money-back guarantee, the client is much more willing to pay for testing.

Once I've tested a home, the typical homeowner sees the value and is willing to pay a higher price to get the job done right the first time. The original call they made to get a price on equipment they weren't going to buy until a later date has just turned into a sale on an entire system and has moved up by many months. You didn't just give a price on another air conditioner, and you actually eliminated your competitors from ever coming to the table.

The air conditioner became just one part of the sale instead of the focal point of the sale.

Wait, What Just Happened?

So let's go back. When in the imaginary Bill and Sally scenario did you close sale number one? **When Sally saw the need to get her husband involved, she was sold on sale number one.** That is, she was sold on the idea that they needed to do further investigating to solve the problems they were experiencing.

So when did you close sale number two? Sale number two closed shortly after Bill and Sally experienced the test. That's when they decided that value superseded price. At that moment, the job was yours.

Most salespeople would have given up in the first few minutes of that first visit with Sally. They would have decided that Bill and Sally were price shoppers, price shoppers who weren't even ready to buy, at that. It makes sense. Bill and Sally were doing the rational thing: shopping now and buying later. But the thing you need to remember is this: *People buy based on emotion and justify using logic.*

Once Sally began to see that there really was a solution to the issues she was experiencing, all she had to do was tell Bill,

"You need to be here for this meeting," and price was no longer the question.

The Right Process

Every sales call has to have a process, a process that not only fixes the pain your clients are experiencing, but creates value for them. If you want to sell more equipment, then stop focusing on selling boxes! Oddly, as a side benefit, you will also sell more boxes.

Here's the right order for your sales process, whether you are working on sale number one or sale number two:

The Steps to a Winning Sales Process

1) **Engage the Customer's Curiosity.**

2) **Gain Credibility.**

3) **Uncover needs.**

4) **Educate to Enhance Value.**

5) **Offer Solutions (test).**

6) **Close the sale.**

By using the above steps, you'll achieve higher closing ratios, contract more profitable jobs, and end up with much happier customers who will give you great referrals.

Getting Referrals

We have all been told that referrals are the best way to grow business. I agree wholeheartedly that you need to ask for referrals. But for some reason, even satisfied customers are not that great at giving consistent referral business.

Sometimes customers will give you a name or two upon completion of a project, but not all the time. Some companies find it so awkward asking for referrals, they don't even bother. Before I started selling the home-performance way, when I asked for referrals it went something like this:

We would install a new system for a customer and she would be very happy with how the job went. So I'd say, "Sally, I see you're very happy with the work we did for you today. One way we grow our business is by asking for referrals. I'm sure you have some friends or neighbors who might be interested in a new air conditioner. Would you mind passing our names on to them?" Sally would give me a "deer in the headlights" look. Then she'd say something like, "Well, I don't know. We really don't talk about this sort of thing when we're visiting friends. But I can see and have them call you."

That all changed when we started testing home performance and finding the real solutions to a customer's underlying problems. Now it's easy to ask: "Sally, we can see that you're very happy with the solutions we provided for you today. We've solved your comfort issues, resolved your high utility bills, and uncovered the real issues that were causing the excessive dust in your home. I'm sure you have some friends and neighbors who would like their homes tested. Would you mind passing our name on to them?"

More often than not, Sally readily says, "Of course," with a big smile on her face.

The big difference is that Sally had problems that affected her daily living, and talking about her daily problems with friends felt perfectly normal to them, especially since her friends likely had the same problems. Sally is thrilled to have the problems solved, and she'll bet her friends would be, too. So of course she's going to talk to them, and when they see how enthusiastic Sally is, of course some of them are going to call us.

When your clients say yes to passing on referrals, you want to assure them that the process will not invade their friends' privacy: "Sally, I don't want you to give me any phone numbers. We're not going to call them. We'd just love it if you ask them to check out our website for more information, or send us an email so we can give them more info, or call us if they're curious about testing."

If you do that, I'm confident that your referral business will grow and grow!

Chapter 7

Turn Service Calls into Paid Opportunities

If you give your service technicians the proper tools, they can actually turn emergency service calls from negative experiences into paid sales leads. All too often service departments are run like fire departments, running around putting fires out. When they are reactive like that, instead of proactive, parts keep breaking down over and over again, with the repercussions of having unhappy customers. Unhappy customers lead to reduced sales, and that you do not want.

Many sales training programs teach technicians how to turn service calls into opportunities to up-sell products or parts. That's not necessarily the best way to turn a service call into a sales opportunity. One problem with this approach is that your technician probably became a tech because he or she did not want to become a salesperson.

Don't get me wrong. Some companies do hire selling techs, or demand that their technicians sell maintenance agreements or look for worn parts and try to up-sell to the homeowner. This can be effective and does bring in extra revenue.

However, I myself would not want someone trying to up-sell me on a service call. I'd much rather hear a technician tell me why the part has failed or what's causing the problem. I'd get a little suspicious if a technician told me that my blower motor is 10 years old and he can give me a discount to replace it since he's already here, or if he told me that it would cost $600 to replace the broken part so he recommends simply putting my money toward a new system. I can read between the lines: He doesn't want to help me solve my problem; he wants to sell me something beyond what I asked for.

On the other hand, if a tech were to tell me, "Your blower motor is running a little high on amps. Since your system is 10 years old, let's consider all your options," then maybe we would have something to talk about.

There are companies out there that use their service department exclusively to up-sell equipment. That's unbelievable! They're not thinking of customer service at all. The technician is programmed to automatically tell the customer that the system is old and the part is $500 to $600, so you should just put the money toward a new system, period.

This is why people are suspicious of heating and cooling contractors in general. They have a reputation for frivolous up-selling. Today's customers are smart, and they appreciate it when you give them information that makes them feel even smarter, not when you try to push them into something they don't need—which can additionally make them feel as if you must think they're stupid. Push hard enough and even if it's something they *do* need, they still might not buy it because they won't trust you.

That's not to say that no customer should ever replace an old system. But if you include customers in the process by educating them, and then only sell them what they truly need, you can stop scaring people off and actually attract more sales. In fact, you can sell the customer solutions that go well beyond a new furnace or air conditioner. But you have to stop thinking in terms of the hard sell, and switch to the idea of education and genuine service.

I'll go so far as to say that almost every call that comes into your business is an opportunity to sell something. Even an existing customer who is calling to complain represents an opportunity to sell more. It's all in how you treat the customer.

"Statistics suggest that when customers complain, business owners and managers ought to get excited about it. The complaining customer represents a huge opportunity for more business." —Zig Ziglar

---

Studies have shown that a vast majority of homeowners who purchased a new high-efficiency furnace or air conditioner would have paid $1,500 more to have the job done right the first time. That's an opportunity for you to make money. In general, service technicians have been trained to find the failed part and replace it, only to be back six to nine months later to find the same part has failed again. Because the system is under warranty, those repairs are usually on your company. That means you're losing money by doing repeated diagnostics to figure out why certain parts keep failing. Warranty work is very expensive for your company, and for the most part you can avoid it by focusing on proper installation in the first place.

I have been on countless service calls where I've discovered that other companies have replaced more parts than you would care to guess at. Often the problem is not that the part or product was poorly made, but that the unit was not properly installed.

Evidence suggests that 95% of premature equipment failure is caused by improper installation and maintenance.

Technicians today go through intensive training to learn how to diagnose failed parts. They have a great understanding of how equipment works. That's why they're technicians.

But one area of failure throughout the industry is that they tend to focus on only one leg of the home system and overlook the other two legs. *Remember, the house is a system with three legs: the shell or envelope is one leg, the duct system is another leg, and the equipment is the third leg.* All three work together. If one leg is broken, then the others have to work that much harder, which causes the weakest link to fail, which oftentimes is the equipment.

Time and time again I've discovered that the failure of an equipment part in one leg of the system could be traced back to one or both of the other legs in the system.

One big problem with many technicians is that they're not doing any testing before or after they repair the equipment.

Perhaps they think testing is a waste of time or money, but in fact, this oversight causes lost revenue and lost customers.

I believe that poor installation and maintenance of equipment and parts is why your business has a "911 season." That is, when the weather turns hot or cold, the phone rings off the hook because the weakest link in the system just failed. Your technician is dispatched to the home to put a Band-Aid on the system, only to return when it fails again during the next 911 season.

Many business owners tell me that their techs can't do much beyond running around doing damage control, because the phone is ringing off the hook. So instead of addressing the underlying issues, they just put more Band-Aids on, in the hope that the customer will maybe choose your company to replace her equipment. But modern customers are too well informed to put up with this sort of patchwork approach for long before they decide you're not the company for them.

Of course, I've also seen homeowners put their own Band-Aids on their homes in an effort to solve their own problems. Haven't you or your technicians seen many an air purifier sitting in a living room and thought, "That guy just wasted lots of money"? But that purifier is another sign that should say to you: Here's a customer with a problem who is willing to pay money to solve it!

Every one of those Band-Aids that homeowners and other contractors have been putting on these problems represents a big opportunity for you to make money. The indoor air quality market is a multibillion-dollar market. And know this: if you don't take your piece of the indoor air quality pie, you have competitors out there who will.

Your Competition Is Not Who You Think

Your biggest competitor is not the one-man-band in a pickup truck or the small shop down the road. No, your new competitors are the big box stores. That's right. They've been listening to your customers' complaints and have discovered an opportunity to make some money. The big box stores aren't stopping there either. They've started marketing to your customers in a whole new way, by stepping out of their doors and into people's homes *just like you do*. Big box stores have recognized the opportunity, and they're responding by offering their own home performance contracting. They're coming after your customers, and if you don't take care of your customers, they will!

If you don't think your customers know about home performance contracting—think again! It's all over the Internet: the latest news about why you should test your home before you install anything. Never ever underestimate your customers' intelligence. It doesn't pay.

Do Up-sell, But Don't Guess

There's nothing wrong with up-selling in and of itself. Many industries do it, and the extra products sold often serve the needs of the customer. But up-selling without testing is to the home heating and cooling industry as malpractice is to the medical field.

If you want to keep your customers, grow your business with great referrals, and be more profitable, you need to change the way your technicians perform service calls. You might be thinking, "But we have happy customers. They do give us referrals." That may be true, but it's unlikely you have anywhere close to as many happy customers or referrals as you might have. The Department of Energy says nine out of ten homes have indoor air quality (IAQ) problems. That's over 90% of your customers! Are over 90% of your customers raving about your solutions to their problems?

So now you might be setting up another mental roadblock, thinking, "But we're not getting that many IAQ calls." I believe you. *That's exactly the problem: you're not marketing, or even talking about, indoor air quality.* You're still in product-selling mode. You need to switch to educating mode.

What would happen if you started asking homeowners if they're experiencing uncomfortable rooms, asthma and allergy problems, high energy bills, or dust issues in their home? What would happen if you started telling them that you have real solutions to these issues? I don't mean by guessing, but by doing a home and duct performance test that will actually diagnose their issues in a measurable way. I'll tell you what would happen: You would up-sell like crazy without having to apply Band-Aid after Band-Aid, and without having to hard-sell your clients.

Don't Guess. Test!

We've talked about the steps for an effective sales call, so we don't need to reinvent the wheel here. However, up-selling at a service call is a slightly different scenario. Your final goal is the same: to uncover your customers' pain and pique their curiosity so they want to further investigate more comprehensive solutions. But because they called for service, you must give them that, too. How do you juggle both?

This is a service call, so we can assume that your customer trusts your technician when it comes to diagnosing a failed air conditioner or furnace. If not, another company would have been called. The customer knows that the person you've sent to help is a technician and trained to fix these sorts of problems. What consumers don't like is when a technician starts to sell them on new equipment or accessories when what they requested was a repair.

On the other hand, most homeowners don't mind being offered a maintenance plan on their equipment. They can usually see the sense in taking care of the equipment they buy. But what happens all too often is that a technician sells the customer a maintenance plan, and then when *any problem of any kind* arrives, the customer assumes it should be covered under the plan.

Think about it. You sell a maintenance plan in the spring on a piece of equipment you know little about. You clean and service the equipment just like the plan says. On the hottest day that summer, you get a call saying that the AC doesn't work. Your technician goes out to the home and finds out the coil has frozen up. Through diagnostic testing, he discovers that the return air is too small, which is what's causing the coil to freeze. He tells the customers that they need to cut in some more return airs to solve the freezing coil. Right away the customers say, "You were just here in the spring and serviced it. Why now do we have this problem? It never did this before!"

How do you know if it never did this before? You have no idea what it did before. You assumed it was always working because the homeowner never offered any information about it. Maybe it never did do this before. But it did it after you arrived, so now you're declared guilty by default.

I'm sure you've experienced the above scenario more than once. We all have. Doesn't it make you wish you had done some checking when you were out there the first time? Warranty work sucks when it's on your dime, doesn't it? In this sort of situation, if you don't offer some type of concession, you'll probably lose a maintenance customer. Because for him, if he paid extra for a maintenance plan hoping it would make the equipment worry-free for the next 10 years, and he still has to pay to fix it now, then the value just went out the window.

When my business started doing the proper testing procedures, starting with the service call, we cut our warranty work by 50%. Not only did we see less warranty work, we also saw more leads coming from the service department, which led to more sales, not to mention happier customers.

If you want to increase customer satisfaction, if you want to sell more maintenance agreements, if you want to get more quality leads with an 80 to 90 % closing ratio—then stop pushing your techs to up-sell on potential problem parts. Instead, *teach them to test, not guess.*

Many of you have checklists and questionnaires that you go through with your customers. But they probably aren't helping you, because you're not approaching them right.

A Typical Checklist of Questions for Customers

- **Do you have any cold or hot spots in your home?**
- **Are your utility bills too high?**
- **Are you having dust issues in your home?**
- **Are you happy with your existing equipment?**

You've been trained to ask the above questions on the front side of the service call, hoping the customer will spill the beans and give you an opportunity to try selling him a filter, UV light, thermostat, or some other add-on sale. Some contractors have been successful with this approach. Others don't bother because they feel awkward or don't have the gift of gab. Or when the 911 season starts, they quit asking these questions because they don't have time; they're too busy putting Band-Aids on broken systems.

Success lies in sales systems that have a purpose that benefits both parties! If customers listen to your systematic approach and can't hear what's in it for them, it will come across as a sales gimmick. By the same token, if your technician doesn't see how it will benefit his performance as a technician, he too will think it's a sales gimmick.

That's why the home performance approach outshines every other approach, with lasting results. You actually diagnose the real cause of the failed part, so that you can educate the homeowner with concrete information. Then the homeowner feels ownership in the solution: having the option to repair it, leave it, or address the larger underlying issues.

Another benefit is that testing also empowers the technician, allowing him or her to find out if the customer has any undiagnosed problems and to ask all those up-sell questions from a position of knowledge—after doing the diagnostic testing, not before.

Remember, more than 90% of your customers have problems that go beyond what they called about. This is your opportunity to uncover those bigger problems, offer real solutions, and gain credibility for future opportunities.

Your New, Improved Service Call

Let's take the systematic approach on the road. I'm about to demonstrate for you how to run a service call that becomes a real sales opportunity. The service call for this scenario will be an emergency call from a customer who has no heat. The customer called in with the following information:

Name: Bill Brown
Address: 1000 Elm Street, Any Town
Equipment: Natural gas 90+ forced air furnace
Air Conditioning: Yes
Age of equipment: 10+ years
House: Two-story with one heating system.
No zoning that we know of.
Previous service: Not known

To set the scene for the service call, we'll assume that you're the technician. You've made a pre-appointment call to say you're on the way, parked on the road outside the home, checked to make sure you're at the right house, introduced yourself to the homeowner, and entered the home wearing booties and using drop cloths. This time the homeowner you're dealing with is Bill, instead of his wife, Sally. Let's start from the point when you're ready to head to the home's malfunctioning equipment to check it:

You: Bill, if you could show me where the furnace is, I'll find the solution to your no-heat situation.

Bill: Great! It's right this way.

135

Once Bill shows you where the furnace is, you start your diagnostic testing to find the failed part that's preventing Bill's home from getting heat. For this scenario, let's say the inducer motor is the failed part. Once you've figured that out, you go find Bill and bring him to the furnace to show him what has failed. You explain what the cost would be to replace the inducer.

So far, this service call probably seems much like any other service call you've done before. But here's where it starts to shift. You're also going to explain the following:

You: Bill, I'm not sure why the inducer failed, but when I get the heat back on I'll do some further testing to see if I can find the cause. Once the inducer motor is in and the house is heating back up, I'll perform three tests on your system. Here are the three tests I'm going to do (remember, customers want to be educated and informed and to feel they're in on the process):

Test One is a static test across the furnace. This is like taking the blood pressure of the system. We know that a typical forced air heating system will run around a half inch of static pressure, which we measure in terms of water column, or WC. If I'm getting a higher reading, say .9 or 1.2-inches of WC, then I'll know that could be one of the culprits that caused the inducer to fail.

Test Two will be taking a temperature rise. This will tell you what the temperature of your furnace is. It is like taking the temperature of your body; if it's too high you are sick. The furnace should be at a 30 to 60 degree temperature rise.

Test Three will make sure you're getting complete combustion of flue gasses. This test will tell me how efficiently the furnace is operating, how much oxygen it's using, and whether it's generating dangerous levels of carbon monoxide (CO).

Let's say your test results are these:

> **Static test:** 1.2 WC
> **Temperature Rise:** 75 deg.
> **Combustion test:** CO 15ppm, Oxygen 9.8%, Efficiency 91.5%

Once you have the heat back on, you come back to Bill and say: "Bill, the heat is on!" It's important that you address that first, so Bill recognizes that you made it a priority to give him the emergency service he asked for. But now that the emergency is over, you have a chance to gain mindshare with the customer. Remember, you did tell Bill you were going to do some further testing. So he won't be surprised now if you want to discuss the results, which is the subject you broach next:

You: Bill, I did some further testing on your heating system to see if I could find the reason the inducer motor failed. Do you mind if I ask you a couple of specifics about you and your home? This may help me understand my test results.

What's Bill going to say? "No, you can't ask me any questions"? Of course not! He's eager to find out what caused the part to fail and willing to answer some questions. Here is where you'll ask your pain questions—never *before* you solve the emergency, only *after*. That's where so many companies lose the up-sell, because they ask a bunch of questions on the front side of a service call. The customer is put off, immediately suspicious that you don't care about his problem and only want to sell him something. But it doesn't have to be an either-or proposition.

You just have to be better at communicating that you really want to help them solve their problems. Then it will be easier to sell them something to solve their problems.

The questions you ask should always correlate with the test results you've taken. If the furnace is running high static, you can be pretty sure that Bill has uncomfortable rooms. This can also indicate duct leakage, which may be causing health issues because of unnecessary dust and allergens floating around his home. If the temperature rise is high, which a dirty filter can make even worse, that can cause not only comfort issues but also higher energy bills. When you ask the following questions, Bill will answer them based on what he knows about his home. Let him explain in his own way. Remember: Bill lives in this home and he knows the issues.

"Bill...

1. In the summer time which rooms are the warmest?

2. In the wintertime which rooms are the coldest?

3. Does your furniture seem to get dusty again just a few days after cleaning?

4. Does your heating or cooling system ever run non-stop but still not keep you comfortable?

5. How important is it to you to save money on your energy bill?

6. Does anyone in your house suffer from asthma or allergies?

7. Does anyone in your house get frequent headaches or flu-like symptoms or feel tired all the time?

8. What is one thing in particular that you don't like about your heating and cooling system?"

For this scenario, let's say that Bill has uncomfortable rooms. Here are a few more things he might tell you:

Bill: In fact, my whole second story is too cold. Sally complains all the time about the house being dusty. She says it leaves her stuffy and she gets a lot of sinus infections. And I talked to a friend of mine who has a house about the same size as mine, but it seems like his energy bills are a lot smaller than mine.

Here's how you might effectively explain the way that Bill's answers relate to your test results:

You: Bill, the test results that I got from your equipment really explain why you're experiencing the problems you've described. Your furnace should be running around a half inch of static. My tests show that it's running much higher than that. That means your furnace will have a hard time sending heat where it's supposed to go, like the second story. You might not know this, Bill, but duct leakage can also contribute to that sort of efficiency problem, causing high energy bills. Leaky ducts also cause excessive dust. The Department of Energy says a typical leaky duct system can cost you 20% to 40% of the energy you pay for to heat and cool your home.

Bill, we can leave the system the way it is—you do have heat now. But there's a very good chance that the inducer will fail again.

What I would recommend is that we do a home-and-duct performance test on your home. This test was invented by scientists from the Department of Energy. What we'll do is put an infiltrometer blower door in your doorway. We'll use that to bring your home into a negative pressure. It's like having a 15-mile-an-hour wind on all four sides of your home at the same time, which won't hurt your home, but will show us how well your system is working. This test will not only answer the mystery of the issues you're experiencing, but it will also give us some great solutions for fixing them. Does this make sense?

Now, we do charge for the test, but it comes with a 100% risk-free guarantee. If you see no value when we're done testing, you don't have to pay us!

If Bill agrees, and my experience tells me he will, you simply ask what day works best for him. If Bill turns the test down, you've informed him that the part will probably fail again. That means—get this—you no longer have to do warranty work on the part when it fails in the next 911 season. If it fails again, it's on *him*!

The biggest differences with this approach versus up-selling on potentially worn-out parts are: 1) you truly did uncover Bill's pain, rather than just handing him another Band-Aid, and 2) you put him in control of deciding how far he wanted to take solving that pain. Bill knows you have the solutions, and he can see the value of investing in a whole-house test.

Testing Genuinely Helps Your Customers

Marketing and selling to generate the average lead in today's market can cost a business about $300 to $600 per lead. Why pay that, when you can turn your service calls into no-cost leads? In fact, with the approach I've described, you're actually getting paid to bring in a good lead!

Should your technicians be doing a combustion test on every gas furnace they service? *Of course!* You'd be crazy not to. If you're servicing gas equipment and you're *not* performing a combustion test, you're opening a door to an enormous potential liability for your company. Carbon monoxide is colorless, odorless, and tasteless. So how in the world do you know if it's there unless you test for it?

A contractor once told me, "We don't do that test. We just clean and service the equipment. Our maintenance agreement does not say we'll do that test." So what? Is that going to stop him from getting sued? Or worse, *killing someone*?

Failing to test a system really can result in someone's death!

Let me tell you a sad story. Back in the early 1990s, I was called out to a house to service the furnace. The homeowner was selling the home, and the potential buyer wanted to make sure the heating equipment was safe. I went through the system and everything checked out fine, *until I checked the flue gasses for carbon monoxide.* The CO levels were so high that I shut the system off before explaining the situation to the homeowner and laying out his options. In his case, the equipment was over 20 years old, so I suggested he was probably better off putting any money towards a new furnace. This thing really was on its last leg.

He was upset because he had already put so much money into the house and didn't want to spend any more. So I pulled out a tag and asked him to sign the bottom, acknowledging that the furnace was not safe to run in its current condition. When he refused to sign it, I wrote on a form that the customer refused to sign, collected my service fee, and left.

That winter, a one-year-old and a three-year-old died in that house from carbon monoxide poisoning!

The sheriff's department found out I had been at the home, so they called me. They wanted records of what I did. It's a good thing for me that I had those records!

Now imagine if I had the attitude that other contractor shared with me: "We don't do that test... Our maintenance agreement does not say we'll do that test." Do you think that would have been an adequate explanation for the sheriff? Not on your life! When I gave the sheriff's office copies of my test results, I was considered a professional who did all he could do. I was still upset that the homeowner hadn't listened to me. But I had done my best.

If that story doesn't wake contractors up, I don't know what will. Some of these problems don't just make people uncomfortable. They can kill people. And you're the one working on their equipment, which can make you responsible.

If you're not testing on every call, you're nuts!

Combustion testing should be a standard procedure for every call you go on, for the safety of your customers and to prevent any liability to your company. Over 50,000 people a year go to the emergency room for at least low levels of carbon monoxide poisoning. The first signs are always feeling tired and experiencing flu-like symptoms.

Every home should have working carbon monoxide alarms, even if it doesn't have gas appliances. If there is an attached garage, that can also contribute to carbon monoxide levels in the home. Every time the garage door opens it's like a tracheotomy into the house. Everything we don't want in our house, we put in the garage—for a reason.

Let's recap this procedure:

Basic Tests You Should Offer on Every Service Call:

- **Static Test**
- **Combustion Test**
- **Temperature Rise Test**

Start doing the above standard tests on every call and you'll see real results that reward both you and your customers.

"But We Don't Have Time"

You might be thinking, "That's great, but when it's 100 degrees out or 40 below zero, my technicians can't spend that much time on a call." There's some truth to that, but you still need to at least do the basic testing. You don't have to hang around for a long conversation, but you can still set the stage for a follow-up call like this:

> **You:** Bill, I did get the heat back on and I did a static test on your system and I'm a little concerned about the static test—that blood pressure test I explained. If we leave the system the way it is, the part I just installed will probably fail again. Right now I have many customers who are out of heat like you, so I don't have time to do further testing today, and the system is safe to run for now. But I strongly recommend we come back for further testing. Would you

like me to have one of our comfort specialists call you to further discuss this?"

Nine times out of ten, Bill will agree to another call. Now you have a great lead to follow up on when the 911 season is over, and your customer won't feel put upon. In fact, he'll probably thank you for it. That's just one more way to separate yourself from your competitors, by solving the real issues your customers are experiencing.

If you chase a purpose, money will chase you. And if you're in a service industry, then shouldn't your purpose be to offer the best customer service around? You don't have to push up-selling to get bigger tickets. When you do the right thing, the rewards are real.

Chapter 8

A New Beginning

Top performers aren't 100 percent better in any one area.
They're one percent better in hundreds of areas."
– Thomas Freese

D o you really have to change the way you're doing business?
Only if you want to change your results! I guarantee you
that your customers have changed. Many of them are not
satisfied with the results they've received in the past 10 to
15 years.

A study by Decision Analyst Incorporated found that an
alarming three out of ten new equipment installations required
the contractors to return to the home before the system would
run properly. Often the problem was that they didn't adequately
explain the system's operation when they installed it. The study
also found that 53% of customers weren't seeing the energy
savings they expected. What's more, 52% said that not all
their rooms were receiving the improved cooling or heating
they expected.

Don't let those figures scare you. Instead, let them motivate
you. If improper installation is a major mistake of most contractors, isn't it exciting to know that you can already begin
to set yourself apart simply by doing things right the first
time? The opportunities are at your fingertips. All you have
to do is take advantage of them.

I have a good friend who owns a plumbing company, and he has been extremely successful with implementing great sales systems. I remember a conversation I had with him about new opportunities in the marketplace. He told me he was thinking about adding a heating division to his plumbing business. I encouraged him to do it, saying I thought it would be a great fit. When he made the switch, I coached and trained his employees to look for and recognize all the opportunities in any service call. The results they've seen are phenomenal!

Let me share the results that one of his top-performing technicians was able to achieve simply by educating a homeowner about all the options:

This tech went on a service call to help a customer who had a leaky water heater. It was obvious the customer needed a new water heater. The technician followed the steps from my training program, asking the right questions to find out what the customer really needed. Of course, the customer's immediate concern was stopping the leak. So the technician took care of that first.

The technician could see that putting in a new water heater would solve the leak. This would mean changing out the old 50-gallon heater for a new 50-gallon heater. By asking further probing questions, the technician found out that the homeowner was also very interested in saving energy. This led to him telling the customer about a new on-demand water heater, and the customer decided to buy that higher-end product. But the visit didn't end there.

Once the on-demand water heater was installed the emergency was over. But the tech understood that by solving the customer's problem, he had gained mindshare. Now was his opportunity to expand on that. The technician asked some further questions about the customer's experience of his home and found out that he had more problems.

The tech then used the customer's answers as a bouncing board to explain the other services their company offered that might help solve his problems. The homeowner's problems included uncomfortable rooms, high utility bills, and excessive dust.

Upon explaining what might be behind the problems the customer was experiencing, the tech sold him on a whole-house test. That testing uncovered all the problems the customer was experiencing, and the technician was ready to offer real solutions. The customer was sold on those solutions, which landed the company a $98,000 project, including: the attic, the crawlspace, duct replacement, equipment replacement, and a bathroom remodel.

That all happened just because the technician asked—at the right moment of course.

The customer was so happy he told his friends, which yielded the company another $270,000 in referral work in the next 10 months. *All from one leaky-heater service call!*

I'll agree that stories like that won't happen every day when you change the way you do business. But they will happen more often. And if you don't start educating your customers, you're walking past thousands of dollars in untapped business. Maybe not every new job you land will be worth tens of thousands of dollars, but you will land a lot more jobs. What would a 10% higher closing ratio mean to you? That's the kind of potential I'm talking about.

Sooner or later those people are going to get someone to fix their home system problems. Why shouldn't it be you? If you're sitting around half the year waiting for extreme weather to make the phone start ringing, and the other half running around putting fires out—why? You don't have to. If you're spending hard-earned money to advertise promotions to create more work, only to have your competitors offer the same thing—why? You don't have to. You can generate more business simply by educating your customers, asking questions, and giving them the opportunity to solve the problems nobody else is talking to them about.

If you've read this far, your next question is probably, "Okay, if I'm ready to change, then what's my first step?" Great! I'll break this down step by step:

Three Steps to Revolutionize Your Business:

1) **Write down your goals.** Start by answering the questions I gave you in Chapter One to help you identify your short-term and long-term goals. Make sure to give yourself a timetable in which to achieve them. I recommend you find a coach to help you start the process. If you don't know where to find a coach, I can help!

2) **Get educated about building science and the whole-house approach.**

3) **Have all your technicians automatically give customers the three diagnostic tests: static test, combustion test, and temperature rise test.** This will start the process of learning why a part

has failed so they can begin educating the customer. This will make your company stand out from the competition, and will immediately start funneling a larger revenue stream into your service department.

Remember, you don't have to change everything all at once. Start slow and steady, but be consistent and track the results. Not only will you have happier customers and make more money, you'll also have the satisfaction of knowing that you're no longer just giving customers the bare minimal solutions to get by. You're actually helping them solve important problems—with solutions many of them didn't even know were possible. Imagine that: you can own a business that makes more money by making a difference! What are you waiting for?

Arne Raisanen
Business Coach
Battleground, WA 98604
360-609-9647
arne@arbco.us
www.arbcci.com

CPSIA information can be obtained
at www.ICGtesting.com
Printed in the USA
FSOW02n1835240516
20752FS